Sequencing Apple's DNA

# Sequencing Apple's DNA

Patrick Corsi
Dominique Morin

WILEY

First published 2016 in Great Britain and the United States by ISTE Ltd and John Wiley & Sons, Inc.

ISTE Ltd
27-37 St George's Road
London SW19 4EU
UK

www.iste.co.uk

John Wiley & Sons, Inc.
111 River Street
Hoboken, NJ 07030
USA

www.wiley.com

Disclaimer
The purpose of this book is to educate and entertain. The author or publisher does not guarantee that anyone following the techniques, suggestions, tips, ideas or strategies will become successful. The author and the publisher shall have neither liability nor responsibility to anyone with respect to any loss or damage caused or alleged to be caused, directly or indirectly, by the information contained in this book.

Library of Congress Control Number: 2015955796

British Library Cataloguing-in-Publication Data
A CIP record for this book is available from the British Library
ISBN 978-1-84821-919-9

# Contents

Acknowledgments . . . . . . . . . . . . . . . . . . . . . . . . . . . . . . . .   xi

Preface . . . . . . . . . . . . . . . . . . . . . . . . . . . . . . . . . . . . .   xiii

Introduction . . . . . . . . . . . . . . . . . . . . . . . . . . . . . . . . . .   xxvii

Part 1. From Insanely Successful Episodes . . . . . . . . . . . . . . . . . . .   1

Chapter 1. Sequencing the First Segments of Apple's DNA . . . . . . . . . .   3

  1.1. The gene, domain and cultural bias . . . . . . . . . . . . . . . . . . . . . .   3
  1.2. Nine DNA segments of rare importance . . . . . . . . . . . . . . . . . . . . .   4

Chapter 2. On Risk Taking . . . . . . . . . . . . . . . . . . . . . . . . . . .   7

  2.1. Where is the gap? . . . . . . . . . . . . . . . . . . . . . . . . . . . . . . .   7
    2.1.1. Business school . . . . . . . . . . . . . . . . . . . . . . . . . . . . .   7
    2.1.2. Apple . . . . . . . . . . . . . . . . . . . . . . . . . . . . . . . . . .   8
  2.2. Amplifying the gap and progressing . . . . . . . . . . . . . . . . . . . . . .   9
  2.3. The genes . . . . . . . . . . . . . . . . . . . . . . . . . . . . . . . . . . .   13

Chapter 3. Product Design . . . . . . . . . . . . . . . . . . . . . . . . . . .   15

  3.1. Where is the gap? . . . . . . . . . . . . . . . . . . . . . . . . . . . . . . .   15
    3.1.1. Business school . . . . . . . . . . . . . . . . . . . . . . . . . . . . .   15
    3.1.2. Apple . . . . . . . . . . . . . . . . . . . . . . . . . . . . . . . . . .   16
  3.2. Amplifying the gap and progressing . . . . . . . . . . . . . . . . . . . . . .   16
    3.2.1. On packing with functionality . . . . . . . . . . . . . . . . . . . . . .   18

Chapter 4. Market Studies . . . . . . . . . . . . . . . . . . . . . . . . . . .   21

  4.1. Where is the gap? . . . . . . . . . . . . . . . . . . . . . . . . . . . . . . .   21

4.1.1. Business school . . . . . . . . . . . . . . . . . . . . . . . . . . . .    21

4.1.2. Apple. . . . . . . . . . . . . . . . . . . . . . . . . . . . . . . . . .    22

4.2. Amplifying the gap and progressing . . . . . . . . . . . . . . . . . . .    22

**Chapter 5. Giving up Some Fights** . . . . . . . . . . . . . . . . . . . .    25

5.1. The chasm . . . . . . . . . . . . . . . . . . . . . . . . . . . . . . . .    25

5.1.1. Business school . . . . . . . . . . . . . . . . . . . . . . . . . . . .    25

5.1.2. Apple. . . . . . . . . . . . . . . . . . . . . . . . . . . . . . . . . .    26

5.2. Amplifying the gap and progressing . . . . . . . . . . . . . . . . . . .    26

**Chapter 6. Entering New Markets** . . . . . . . . . . . . . . . . . . . .    29

6.1. The chasm . . . . . . . . . . . . . . . . . . . . . . . . . . . . . . . .    29

6.1.1. Business school . . . . . . . . . . . . . . . . . . . . . . . . . . . .    29

6.1.2. Apple. . . . . . . . . . . . . . . . . . . . . . . . . . . . . . . . . .    30

6.2. Amplifying the gap and progressing . . . . . . . . . . . . . . . . . . .    30

**Chapter 7. Apple, the Learning Company** . . . . . . . . . . . . . . . .    33

7.1. The chasm . . . . . . . . . . . . . . . . . . . . . . . . . . . . . . . .    33

7.1.1. Business school . . . . . . . . . . . . . . . . . . . . . . . . . . . .    34

7.1.2. Apple. . . . . . . . . . . . . . . . . . . . . . . . . . . . . . . . . .    34

7.2. Amplifying the gap and progressing . . . . . . . . . . . . . . . . . . .    35

**Chapter 8. On Research and Development.** . . . . . . . . . . . . . . . .    39

8.1. The chasm . . . . . . . . . . . . . . . . . . . . . . . . . . . . . . . .    39

8.1.1. Business school . . . . . . . . . . . . . . . . . . . . . . . . . . . .    40

8.1.2. Apple. . . . . . . . . . . . . . . . . . . . . . . . . . . . . . . . . .    40

8.2. Amplifying the gap and progressing . . . . . . . . . . . . . . . . . . .    40

**Chapter 9. On Company Acquisition** . . . . . . . . . . . . . . . . . . .    45

9.1. The chasm . . . . . . . . . . . . . . . . . . . . . . . . . . . . . . . .    45

9.1.1. Business school . . . . . . . . . . . . . . . . . . . . . . . . . . . .    45

9.1.2. Apple. . . . . . . . . . . . . . . . . . . . . . . . . . . . . . . . . .    46

9.2. Amplifying the gap . . . . . . . . . . . . . . . . . . . . . . . . . . . .    46

9.3. Progressing the gap . . . . . . . . . . . . . . . . . . . . . . . . . . .    52

**Chapter 10. The Manager, the  Software and the Process** . . . . . . . . . . .    55

10.1. The chasm. . . . . . . . . . . . . . . . . . . . . . . . . . . . . . . .    55

10.1.1. Business school way . . . . . . . . . . . . . . . . . . . . . . . . .    55

10.1.2. Apple's way . . . . . . . . . . . . . . . . . . . . . . . . . . . . . .    56

10.2. Developing the chasm . . . . . . . . . . . . . . . . . . . . . . . . . .    56

10.2.1. The case of Mister Hullot. . . . . . . . . . . . . . . . . . . . . . . . .    57
10.2.2. Drawing lessons from software management . . . . . . . . . . . . . . .    58

**Part 2. Emergence of a Brand: From Failures to
Everyday Situations (In Search of Exclusive Value)** . . . . . . . . . . . .    61

**Chapter 11. Failures Left Behind** . . . . . . . . . . . . . . . . . . . . . . . .    63

11.1. Why failures? . . . . . . . . . . . . . . . . . . . . . . . . . . . . . . .    63
11.1.1. Business school . . . . . . . . . . . . . . . . . . . . . . . . . . . . .    63
11.1.2. Apple . . . . . . . . . . . . . . . . . . . . . . . . . . . . . . . . . .    63
11.2. Failure dissolves in time . . . . . . . . . . . . . . . . . . . . . . . . . .    64
11.3. A basket of historical failures . . . . . . . . . . . . . . . . . . . . . . .    64

**Chapter 12. A Cornucopia of Commerce Situations** . . . . . . . . . . . .    71

12.1. Commercial policy . . . . . . . . . . . . . . . . . . . . . . . . . . . . .    71
12.1.1. Business school . . . . . . . . . . . . . . . . . . . . . . . . . . . . .    71
12.1.2. Apple . . . . . . . . . . . . . . . . . . . . . . . . . . . . . . . . . .    71
12.2. Asking customers . . . . . . . . . . . . . . . . . . . . . . . . . . . . .    71
12.2.1. Business school . . . . . . . . . . . . . . . . . . . . . . . . . . . . .    71
12.2.2. Apple . . . . . . . . . . . . . . . . . . . . . . . . . . . . . . . . . .    72
12.2.3. Development . . . . . . . . . . . . . . . . . . . . . . . . . . . . . . .    72
12.3. Forecasting and strategy . . . . . . . . . . . . . . . . . . . . . . . . . .    73
12.3.1. Business school . . . . . . . . . . . . . . . . . . . . . . . . . . . . .    73
12.3.2. Apple . . . . . . . . . . . . . . . . . . . . . . . . . . . . . . . . . .    73
12.3.3. Development . . . . . . . . . . . . . . . . . . . . . . . . . . . . . . .    73
12.4. Grabbing a trend . . . . . . . . . . . . . . . . . . . . . . . . . . . . . .    73
12.4.1. Business school . . . . . . . . . . . . . . . . . . . . . . . . . . . . .    73
12.4.2. Apple . . . . . . . . . . . . . . . . . . . . . . . . . . . . . . . . . .    73
12.4.3. Development . . . . . . . . . . . . . . . . . . . . . . . . . . . . . . .    73
12.5. Communicating . . . . . . . . . . . . . . . . . . . . . . . . . . . . . . .    74
12.5.1. Business school . . . . . . . . . . . . . . . . . . . . . . . . . . . . .    74
12.5.2. Apple . . . . . . . . . . . . . . . . . . . . . . . . . . . . . . . . . .    74
12.5.3. Development . . . . . . . . . . . . . . . . . . . . . . . . . . . . . . .    74
12.6. Getting incomparable value . . . . . . . . . . . . . . . . . . . . . . . .    74
12.6.1. Business school . . . . . . . . . . . . . . . . . . . . . . . . . . . . .    74
12.6.2. Apple . . . . . . . . . . . . . . . . . . . . . . . . . . . . . . . . . .    74
12.6.3. Development . . . . . . . . . . . . . . . . . . . . . . . . . . . . . . .    75
12.7. Making something profitable . . . . . . . . . . . . . . . . . . . . . . . .    75
12.7.1. Business school . . . . . . . . . . . . . . . . . . . . . . . . . . . . .    75
12.7.2. Apple . . . . . . . . . . . . . . . . . . . . . . . . . . . . . . . . . .    75
12.7.3. Development . . . . . . . . . . . . . . . . . . . . . . . . . . . . . . .    75
12.8. Going after the enterprise market . . . . . . . . . . . . . . . . . . . . .    75

12.8.1. Business school . . . . . . . . . . . . . . . . . . . . . . . . . . . . 75

12.8.2. Apple . . . . . . . . . . . . . . . . . . . . . . . . . . . . . . . . . . 76

12.8.3. Development . . . . . . . . . . . . . . . . . . . . . . . . . . . . . . 76

12.9. Expenses versus returns . . . . . . . . . . . . . . . . . . . . . . . . . 76

12.9.1. Business school . . . . . . . . . . . . . . . . . . . . . . . . . . . . 76

12.9.2. Apple . . . . . . . . . . . . . . . . . . . . . . . . . . . . . . . . . . 76

12.9.3. Development . . . . . . . . . . . . . . . . . . . . . . . . . . . . . . 76

12.10. Management to commitment to product . . . . . . . . . . . . . . . . 77

12.10.1. Business school . . . . . . . . . . . . . . . . . . . . . . . . . . . 77

12.10.2. Apple . . . . . . . . . . . . . . . . . . . . . . . . . . . . . . . . . 77

12.10.3. Development . . . . . . . . . . . . . . . . . . . . . . . . . . . . . 77

Chapter 13. Emergence of a Brand . . . . . . . . . . . . . . . . . . . . . . 79

13.1. The chasm . . . . . . . . . . . . . . . . . . . . . . . . . . . . . . . . . 79

13.1.1. Business school . . . . . . . . . . . . . . . . . . . . . . . . . . . . 79

13.1.2. Apple . . . . . . . . . . . . . . . . . . . . . . . . . . . . . . . . . . 80

13.2. Amplifying the gap and progressing . . . . . . . . . . . . . . . . . . 81

Part 3. Importing Apple's Genes into Transferable
Knowledge (In Evidence of Deeper Gaps) . . . . . . . . . . . . . . . . . 83

Chapter 14. On Structure and Contents . . . . . . . . . . . . . . . . . . . 85

14.1. The chasm . . . . . . . . . . . . . . . . . . . . . . . . . . . . . . . . . 85

14.1.1. Business school . . . . . . . . . . . . . . . . . . . . . . . . . . . . 85

14.1.2. Apple . . . . . . . . . . . . . . . . . . . . . . . . . . . . . . . . . . 86

14.2. Developing the chasm . . . . . . . . . . . . . . . . . . . . . . . . . . . 86

Chapter 15. You Said Reality? Which Reality? . . . . . . . . . . . . . . . 89

15.1. The chasm . . . . . . . . . . . . . . . . . . . . . . . . . . . . . . . . . 89

15.1.1. Business school . . . . . . . . . . . . . . . . . . . . . . . . . . . . 90

15.1.2. Apple . . . . . . . . . . . . . . . . . . . . . . . . . . . . . . . . . . 90

15.2. Developing the chasm . . . . . . . . . . . . . . . . . . . . . . . . . . . 92

15.3. It's all about perception . . . . . . . . . . . . . . . . . . . . . . . . . . 95

Chapter 16. Combining the Genes . . . . . . . . . . . . . . . . . . . . . . . 99

16.1. Taking stock of a flat list of genes . . . . . . . . . . . . . . . . . . . 99

16.2. Setting the stage toward a combined dynamics . . . . . . . . . . . . 103

16.2.1. In search for dominant designs . . . . . . . . . . . . . . . . . . . 103

16.2.2. Breaking the dominant designs . . . . . . . . . . . . . . . . . . . 104

16.2.3. Blueprinting radical "crazy" concepts . . . . . . . . . . . . . . . 105

**Chapter 17. Evolving Competition** . . . . . . . . . . . . . . . . . . . . . . . . .    107

17.1. Cracking open the notion of "competition"   . . . . . . . . . . . . . . . .    107
17.2. Designing an expanded understanding "competition"   . . . . . . . . . . .    109

**Chapter 18. Evolving Innovation** . . . . . . . . . . . . . . . . . . . . . . . . .    113

18.1. Cracking open the notion of "innovation"   . . . . . . . . . . . . . . . . .    113
18.2. Designing an expanded understanding of "innovation"   . . . . . . . . . . .    112

**Chapter 19. A Company Under (Dynamic) Tension** . . . . . . . . . . . . . .    117

19.1. Tension is a co-evolving dynamic . . . . . . . . . . . . . . . . . . . . . . .    117
19.2. Tension is a dynamic toward futures . . . . . . . . . . . . . . . . . . . . .    119
19.3. Walking the way . . . . . . . . . . . . . . . . . . . . . . . . . . . . . . . .    120

**Chapter 20. Overcoming Common Blocking Points** . . . . . . . . . . . . . .    123

20.1. The need for an innovation molecule . . . . . . . . . . . . . . . . . . . . .    123
20.2. A need to revisit risk-taking . . . . . . . . . . . . . . . . . . . . . . . . . .    125

**Conclusion** . . . . . . . . . . . . . . . . . . . . . . . . . . . . . . . . . . . . . .    129

**Appendices** . . . . . . . . . . . . . . . . . . . . . . . . . . . . . . . . . . . . . .    133

**Appendix 1** . . . . . . . . . . . . . . . . . . . . . . . . . . . . . . . . . . . . . .    135

**Appendix 2** . . . . . . . . . . . . . . . . . . . . . . . . . . . . . . . . . . . . . .    139

**Appendix 3** . . . . . . . . . . . . . . . . . . . . . . . . . . . . . . . . . . . . . .    151

**Appendix 4** . . . . . . . . . . . . . . . . . . . . . . . . . . . . . . . . . . . . . .    171

**Appendix 5** . . . . . . . . . . . . . . . . . . . . . . . . . . . . . . . . . . . . . .    177

**Appendix 6** . . . . . . . . . . . . . . . . . . . . . . . . . . . . . . . . . . . . . .    187

**Bibliography** . . . . . . . . . . . . . . . . . . . . . . . . . . . . . . . . . . . . .    191

**Index** . . . . . . . . . . . . . . . . . . . . . . . . . . . . . . . . . . . . . . . . .    199

# Acknowledgments

Until recently, we did not know that we would write about Apple. Even though, as young engineers, a formative Apple has tickled our brains and resonated in our hearts since the late 1970s, and even though we have become acute observers of its developments since then.

Yet, no business book could be written without being influenced by special people. We had the opportunity to meet a few individuals having held notable responsibilities within Apple, all of whom were impressive.

One of them was Jean-Marie Hullot, whom we have occasionally hired for training managers in computing projects in the 1980s. Thanks, Jean-Marie, for your very insightful thinking.

Thanks also go to Jean-Louis Gassée who pointed out that Apple, in its darker days, retained a 5% market share, which was not that catastrophic, as it was also the case for BMW!

We personally witnessed the earliest days of both Apple and Microsoft, from Silicon Valley and Europe, and were often tempted to compare their founders' trajectories. Professional circumstances made us switch back and forth in using either IBM PCs or Macintosh architectures and models, sometimes with regrets or awe in front of captivating machines, over 35 years. We joyfully tossed around crazy ideas on the future of the two companies. One day, we even designed a formal-free thinking foresight exercise for graduating students where the trick was to scenarize a number of ventures and business models for an ever expanding Apple until 2030. Coincidence or not, several have come true since. This puzzled us, less so the students probably.

But, for such an improbable book, we had to unknowingly wait until the advent of specific methods to dare crack an Apple conundrum which had puzzled us for so many years. One was C-K theory, another was trialectics, and yet, a first understanding of what makes the distinction between the still predominant linear thinking and what can be dubbed systemic approaches.

Hence, the decoding and interpreting of Apple's DNA components would not have been possible without the power of a special design-thinking method, long since invented and perfected at Mines ParisTech. Our gratitude goes to its Professors Armand Hatchuel, Benoît Weil and Pascal Le Masson and their highly competent team within the *Center de Gestion Scientifique* (Scientific Management Center) for their unfaltering and patient teaching and their sharpest listening through the years. The foundations in designing innovation capacity that they have built are backed by strong theoretical formulations and can now encompass all human activities.

Entering into the arcane of competition and innovation was happily backed by the deep and systematic thinking offered by trialectics. To its founder, Gérard Gigand, our thankful consideration for having generously and diligently instructed the sometimes arcane nuances of his organized mental procedures.

Our gratitude goes to our publisher, and especially Raphaël Ménascé in London, who sensed the feasibility of a genes-based approach.

And finally, a big thank you to our other halves, Annie and Béatrice, who had to wait patiently for the seemingly never-ending final writing touch. You deserve more than a vacation, you deserve the dedication of our silent typing embodied by this book.

## Credits

[CRI 53] The image at front of Part 3 is the historical drawing by artist Ms. Odile Crick (Francis's wife), extracted from: http://hilobrow.com/2011/08/11/odile-crick/ (as of August 2015).

Icon templates are downloaded from: http://www.freevectors.net/details/Application+Icon+Templates.

Icon templates are downloaded from online icon maker: https://FreeIconMaker.com. Images in Part 3 are "Designed by Freepik.com".

Icon made by Freepik from www.flaticon.com.

# Preface

## Setting a new stage

Time is up. Our times require that we transcend the old paradigms of the 20th Century: fixed models, closed systems, linear thinking, etc. Now is the time for new thinking ways: changing the rules, building a genuine consciousness of innovation, acquiring a capacity for sustainability, etc. But, the question is ... *how can we learn?*

In the course of societal and business evolution, sometimes, peculiar elements come to our attention. These may distinguish themselves as a form of a paradigmatic change signaling a distinctive phenomenon; something of particular importance, both unexpected and unprecedented.

A few centuries ago, a host of most creative individuals did what civilization had not seen for many centuries. It sparked from a European region that was not get called Italy yet and spread all over the continent to break free from the conventional, disrupting all domains of knowledge and art, and flourishing to heights in every domain of human endeavor. It was called the Renaissance. It changed the future in ways that were dubbed impossible, even unimaginable before.

Out of that creative wave, one specific man, born in Tuscany, came to show a continuous flow of innovators so varied, so intense, so precise and so structured, that, even today, it just seems impossible from a mere individual. He was named Leonardo as an improbable child, and they just mentioned he came *"da Vinci"*, i.e. from the village of Vinci in beautiful central hilly Tuscany.

A flurry of studies have surrounded Leonardo Da Vinci's works over five centuries – each time surveying through the best lenses of the time – the countless number of domains of human activity which he touched, transformed, transcended and signposted as a remarkable legacy for humanity.

But, a hidden side was left relatively untouched: the *way* of the artifacts, the *thinking way* which underpinned the visible side of the Master.

We were fortunate enough to have been dipped into the family just beneath the Vinci hills at very young age, and returning so many times there, including, in this century, to specifically dig out what we believe to represent a "Leonardo" method. This book provides enough background material about Da Vinci's way we unearthed. And why is this so?

The brief passage on earth of individuals of such caliber results in shaping the world's future (e.g. putting an end to dark medieval times, in the case of Leonardo). But at the same time, it is very hard to be conscious of the real meaning of what was going on during or slightly after his life. Would those few notables having seen the fresh Mona Lisa – *La Gioconda* – painting that Leonardo carried with him throughout his adult life, or the few Dukes and other governing personalities of the time, his civil and military defense master plans, imagine that the creations would still puzzle and awe us today?

By a probable similar token, we feel that the passage of Steve Jobs on this planet signifies another Renaissance yet to come, probably of a different type. We are not speaking of Internet of Things linking up Apple Watches with people and devices. Nor even the iPod and iPad and the many Mac models – although, these are the offspring of a generous and revolutionary *matrix* that bore them. We need to see a wider picture. And for this to happen, to uncover the thinking line which surfaces from time to time, often through citations and speeches, and imprints on our perception.

From Tuscany to the Californian Silicon Valley – two sunny places that are not short of visionary founders despite being 500 years apart – it is not the history that is usually taught officially, but it is the chaos of the human mind that signs off a new era in ways that were simply unimaginable mere decades before. We will provide a number of his citations in Appendix 3 as a way to reveal, piece by piece, the parallel Leonardo–Jobs.

We see these elements as a form of future *"technology tools"*, not assuredly in the sense we would give today to "technology" or to "tools". We may view them as rather abstract perhaps, only because we are not used to thinking in such terms. But, these deep traits are borne out in the recent company's insanely great ascent.

## Why is this book different?

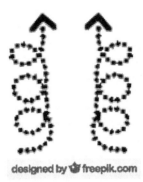

designed by freepik.com

Over the last few years, many books have been published about Apple and its legendary co-founders, and we believe this is just the beginning. Most of them framed the company's fabric as something exceptional or heralded the difficulties, triumphs and despairs of Steven Paul Jobs, his exactness in dealing with visions, plans, form factors and people alike. The story of Apple has already been extensively documented and we provide the main references on the subject in the bibliography.

This book, however, is different: no advice, no ready-made solutions. After all, there are many books, magazines and conferences that bring this ready to use. This book tries to mine the core nuggets which may regenerate a business advantage. By focusing on essential seeds, the postulate is that we can, not merely apply, but originate new concepts, new strategies and new behaviors; food for thought, that is. So, we may become conscious of our own thinking. When we start to be conscious of our thoughts in pursuing business (and, as a matter of fact, just anything), we become able to redraw our plans, change direction or invent whatever new ventures that seem advantageous. We head toward *thought engineering.*

About 10% of this book may be about the genes themselves. And 90% is just comments. Garbage, then? This may not be, as they constitute the instruction manual for activating the genes. The genes are the multi-dimensional embedded substances. They are frequencies. But, these need to be activated, hence the developments supplied. The same as in the DNA, 90% was dubbed "garbage" but seems to be a sort of instruction manual. The strange thing is that the 90% modify the perception – i.e. the understanding – of the 10%: they help us "program" our own way to activate the genes. The engine of transformation requires opening the larger part first.

But so far, very few companies have been able show us the artful way of thinking. We believe to have spotted one such example, hence our proposition to you, dear readers, to investigate how it has faced business. As things evolve, it may well be that what seemed extravagant or crazy a few years ago becomes the norm of the leaders. For this reason, should we not endeavor to analyze and synthesize the findings about such *"wild ducks"?*

Dear readers, we do not think that we have been carried away by Jobs' singularities or as Apple maniacs. Our career spans several industries and companies and we have been accustomed to many environments for more than 70 years combined. Perhaps this makes us more vigilant about what carries more meaning and what may remain as background noise. This book tries to pull impersonal things inside out and reveal what may be hidden behind the visible side, not by disclosing unknown facts for the most part, but in translating the wisdom nuggets into transferable form. If we were to *design* a firm after Apple, would we have to go after yet another Jobs? Or, perhaps, could we mature some consistent knowledge to produce it?

Our future will be populated by vastly different objects, products or services, which we hardly can imagine as yet. Extrapolating from the present is a sure way to fail at some point in time. And we cannot limit our imagination to incremental changes only. What should guide us then? A target value, a divergent thinking, any innovative idea, etc.? Innovation is that odd art of altering the identity of objects. Hence, by opening new categories unsought before, whereby new identities (function and form intertwined into the object) are obtained by warping old ones to various degrees.

Our point is that no ordinary thinking could preside over no less ordinary things. We live in exciting times, in which products and business areas in general, are being reformulated or created. We believe this is just the beginning: there is no limit to the potential of creativity.

## Bridging an Apple capacity for craziness and design innovation

Designed by
freepik.com

This book aims to extract the "molecular genes" leading to craziness. For geniuses design *crazy* things, those things that nobody can *a priori* say are feasible, or are impossible. By crazy, we merely mean *beyond immediate imagination.* No market study is available here to reveal the possibility, for it would necessarily be based on past habits and usage. No viability proof exists yet, for nobody has done it, or even imagined it. And no master plan, roadmap of guidance can be obtained, for nobody has yet seen the path to a result.

We will bring in Leonardo Da Vinci, the Renaissance genius, for two reasons. First, always being fascinated by the Master, we have found over the years that his method of working has striking traits resembling those of Steve Jobs. Most probably not on the same personality or temper level, but rather in terms of *the ways of performing*.

Both had an unmatched gear for innovation, an intense search for perfection, and a special way of linking art and science.

Steve Jobs bringing in Jony Ive's mind the obviousness of "Sunflower design" of the G4 iMac (or iLamp – see caption in Appendix 3) is no different in essence from Leonardo Da Vinci taking inspiration from design solutions (or design patterns, as computer people say) selected by Mother Nature into living organisms, through millions of years of continuous trial and error. To both of them, observing Nature is a privileged way to access to beauty, and superior, elegant and minimalist proven design solutions.

We provide background material on Leonardo's way in Appendix 3 of this book. There is a second reason for calling Da Vinci to help understand Jobs, hence Apple. It is his unique way of designing radically novel concepts, actually quite crazy for his time. For elucidating his special creativity posture, we have to resort to a powerful design innovation method, which is actually backed by mathematical theory. It is called C-K (concepts–knowledge) theory.

A hallmark of the late Steve Jobs was a manifested capacity to cast objects revealing new usages (e.g. the iPod comfortably carrying a flock of songs). Or to irrevocably alter the identity of well-known objects (e.g. the colored plastic or aluminium casings of previously unattractive personal computing embodiments). To stand for, describe, and generalize such indomitable potential, we resolutely called for the authoritative design innovation theory from Mines ParisTech (the famous *Ecole des Mines de Paris*) called C-K (Appendix 4 provides an introduction). A real theory, backed by solid mathematical proof, already exists and is used that can account for the business virtue of a prolific ability to enter unknown crazy domains. We postulated that, by bringing the power of C-K to crack open a number of previous observations we made about Apple, it was possible to trace the genesis of the genes so that they would become transferable across the spectrum of the socioeconomic world. The effects reveal the causes. Genes are a measure of the entity at hand.

This book reveals some of the genetics that lead us to imagining and tackling undecidable things for business and economics.

Although we use a format that opposes that crazy thinking from the classical dominant thinking (and we deliberately use the illustrative example of the archetypal business school type for commodities), the genome that gets under way is no replacement for usual thinking. Nobody would advise us to directly use the genes as they usher in *beyond* the early adopter phase of an innovation adoption process. Some mature markets may prefer the comfort of conservatism, and this can be fine, as long as no disruptive innnovation pops up.

But at times when society is in need of radical adaptation and change for its sustainable pursuit, it is no less than the craziness ability that signs off fresh departures for promising horizons. The sustained art of the difference certainly opposes any complacency. And that formidable capability was chiefly found in Apple, to a yet unmatched degree. We are collectively lucky to witness an exemplar company teaching us the way of the reckless, the path to the fantastic or the gift of the magic. For the crazy way is now in strong demand, and the time has come to share and disseminate elements of that art of the difference.

This book amounts to no conduct guidelines. We remember the IBM Business Conduct Guidelines that we were given on the hiring day at this mythical company in the early 1980s well. Things to do, ways to behave, clear do's and do nots. But here, we strive to build a new consciousness. A consciousness that makes you capable of activating new ways of thinking. It is not dual (do–do not), but anchored on ternary thinking. Figure 1 recalls the relationship between three basic concepts toward completing holistic and sustainable systems [MAS 15] and, beyond, sustaining consciousness itself.

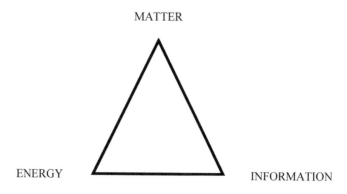

**Figure 1.** *Three dimensions toward realizing a holistic system*

## How to use this book

The *"technology tools"* we provide in this book are meant for executives and strategists, from CEOs to team and project managers and the business practitioner in general.

You may use them in several ways; forging a new way of thinking yields different, better results for your company or projects. This can also regenerate companies. All of them were observed pertaining to the Apple of 1977–2011, when Steve Jobs was in charge and when he was not. By peeling off the layers of a firm's shell (Figure 2) – thus gradually revealing inner conducts – we can get closer to what lies at its root. And in this root Apple's DNA components are located.

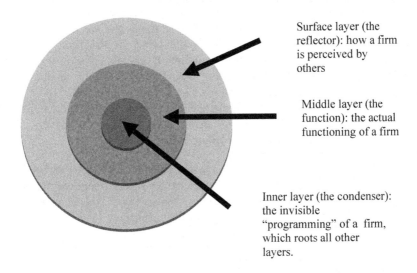

Surface layer (the reflector): how a firm is perceived by others

Middle layer (the function): the actual functioning of a firm

Inner layer (the condenser): the invisible "programming" of a firm, which roots all other layers.

**Figure 2.** *The main layers that form a company's embodiment*

Let us peel off the rings and journey through the layers. The surface layer includes the typical accounting figures, from cash reserves and material assets, as well as the visible side of the firm, its image and its way for getting close to the market. Typically, all components here are public, visible and recordable as imprints on some tangible matter.

The middle layer contains all direct experience and the flows that the firm entertains with its environment. Here lives its metabolism. Knowledge management may be used to explore the decision-making process related to this layer.

There have been few if no key studies on the actual content of the inner layer. We tend to resort to autobiographies, stories about established and other visionaries. Penetrating this layer would be the equivalent of an "introspection" for a human being, thereby raising the same conceptual and practical difficulties. However, here lie the keys to a firm's evolution.

What if we had a tool, or a technology, which could X-ray the three layers? What if we could decode it and linearize its components? Perhaps, we could grasp the very fabric of a particular organization. In fact, the inner layer is the motor of the organization. Acting as a synthetic condenser (of the experiences of the middle layer) first, it squeezes out the lessons, leaving only what is essential. Yet, it retains a dual function, being capable of reproducing that quintessence toward the exterior. It then becomes a propulsion engine in case of need.

This core layer is assimilable to an energy formula and we will use numbered codes to classify them. Another code is the brand of the firm; it is another technology tool that should ideally cross all three layers in a coherent way. It should theoretically be capable of aligning the three layers along one unique outward-oriented axis with three stages:   thinking —> action —> message. To express the value of the inner layer codes for Apple, we will use the market acronym of AAPL, signifying the relation between intrinsic stable power and external floating value and use the DNA segment metaphor for working at them.

To use the book, you may open it up at any page, pick a chapter and go through. Then, please meditate for a while on what excites you: that strangeness that seems to turn things upside down or inside out. For what seemed a peculiar oddness just yesterday may see the light of the day tomorrow morning.

## The power is in the DNA

KEEP DESIGNING.com

There is actually tremendous potential sitting in these DNA segments. As mentioned, they preciously store the inner fabric of a company: what has been learned the hard way and made a deep imprint not to be forgotten by anybody. All this ore constructs piecewise its core values, the firm's nuggets. If and when reawaken properly (i.e. with a sound sense of timing, importance and urgency), they can regenerate the whole firm's body: its middle layer organs and market. However, they are not an advisable cure for any incoming candidate enterprise as their power may clash with ambient cultures if they are not so well aligned.

These DNA tools will be a technology of our future. Perhaps, some researchers will someday find ways to synthesize firms and offer catalogued models of enterprises ready to analyze, classify and even run. As of today, however, we had better resort to and rely on certain people first, especially venture capitalists whose flair senses them well. Perhaps, world leading firms will someday get their DNA sequenced so as to make them more immune to their competitive environment. Or, they will prefer to safeguard their "molecular fabric" in the case of negative disruptions.

We believe that this is exactly what Steve Jobs wanted to do when he began to design Apple University, his in-house program for executives with the mandate to align Apple with the intangible values, ways of thinking, knowledge and other capacities that he regarded as his core legacy. He clearly saw, for instance, when he came back to power in 1995, that the rest of the company (the layers external to the core) was only contingent to the root layer. During his later years, he thus favored targeted case studies, valuable internal and external stories, those which could heartily imprint a lesson in the mind and the heart of the existing and yet to come executive staff. Moreover, are the heart and mind not the "inner layer" of a human being?

Of course, the question is "what do you put in the inner layer?" A genetic mapping is definitely not available today! This book can be viewed as an attempt to populate a "DNA component" which is part of the Apple's inner layer.

We opted to evidence these in a dualistic framework. The reason is that we have had dualities for a long time in our cultures. Hence, we chose the concept of business school to antagonize the components found in an Apple's DNA, respectively, to what a traditional business school long proposed. After all, business schools around the world also represent a dominant thinking of our times.

To be honest, we did meet some business schools that are beyond that reference cliché, and this shows that evolution is possible. But for the most part, we believe the perception of that dominant thinking still persists in the public. So, please see the intended orientation of the antagonism: to foster evolution. By sensing two antagonized extremes, the path will appear easier as it is made clearer. Will the business schools of the future endeavor to forgo some old schemes and bring forth the thinking that perspired through Apple's history?

## How did the authors come up with it?

Perhaps, the answer resides in having two unusual people confronting their own ideas.

For one, Patrick Corsi went to Silicon Valley the day after completing his PhD in computer science at Institut National Polytechnique de Grenoble in France in 1979 to join the then mighty IBM Corp. At that time, mesmerizing trade winds were blowing out of a number of startups forges. And there was Apple blowing fire on your neck, just born out of a devil's cauldron of two young rebels (one more than the other) and a peaceful senior executive who would not last too long. Patrick came back to Europe and joined IBM France a few years later, only to quit 3 years after: was IBM listening to the PC revolution or not quite? He directly embarked on a thorough, famed (and, yes, successful) startup venture in Paris in a then booming artificial intelligence called Cognitech SA.

He had to quit it again, not content with those who bought it out without a clear vision of what artificial intelligence was meant to be someday. After a short management career at Thomson, renamed Thales some time afterward, this is where he met his co-author. Sensing the European construction winds, he could only quit a third time and his co-author Dominique Morin happened to soon succeed him in the job, he joined the European Commission in Brussels.

And lo! A year later, his former successor himself jumped in too for a few years. Catch me if you can, Patrick quit the honorable Commission only a decade later, for not feeling enough of the hot breeze of exciting and singing tomorrows on his neck again. Standing close in spirit to Dominique, he often exchanged views about the lusty firms dominating the computing world. The fact is, in the meantime, a number of trials called Bill Gates himself to come to Brussels and seriously negotiate his Internet Explorer unbundling from an unavoidable Windows operating system.

By then, he began something you cannot quit too easily, an entrepreneurial life, and he started focusing on innovation processes, for all he saw before him spoke of it in one way or another. And he began to think about the art of thinking innovation. Not those cosmetic changes too often confused with innovation, but real *breakthroughs,* so radical that the common belief was to consider them as impossible until they appear. By focusing on what may be left when you peel off all outer rings of any substance matter, he began to notice a few interesting bits that seemed to remain mostly untold yet. He occasionally wrote on innovation and marketing, also on complexity and sustainability, to finally end up contributing to the present book, and (as a tribute to his Italian origins), thereby prone to connecting the "Leonardo Da Vinci" hyper dot to the "Steve Jobs" hyper dot, in the universe of multi-dimensional creativity.

Dominique Morin started his working life in 1977 and terminated it in 2015. He, therefore, belongs to a generation that had the privilege of being witness to Apple's story, from Steve Jobs' parents' garage to becoming the most famous company in the world.

His relationship with Apple has been limited to that of a distant (but attentive) observer, and occasional customer, yet that has been enough to give him, throughout these years, the living experience of its entire rich and complex product history, to date.

Graduating from *Ecole Centrale Paris* (EC 77), in 1977, Dominique Morin had a varied career in the computing world and consulting. He crossed the lines between very small and very large enterprises, from public agency to private business, via the associative world.

He finally settled in aeronautics in the Safran Group by working on the development of embarked critical software, its certification and ultimately the so-called "airworthiness" function, which deals with the demonstration of flight capacity, according to applicable safety regulations. His professional path twice crossed Patrick's, and together they brought to their twinned consciousness a new understanding of things from the side you do not see.

He spends an unreasonable amount of time on various discussion forums dedicated to Apple and is convinced that Apple will have a profound influence on how to approach business issues, which will be documented in many books to come.

One final note: he is an ardent admirer of Frank Zappa too (www.umrk.fr)!

This book is a piecewise contribution, based on our complementary professional experiences. We hope you will have as much fun reading it as we had writing it.

## How is the book structured?

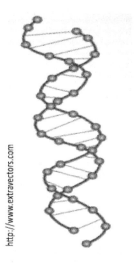

http://www.extravectors.com

The book first provides a series of genes (the so-called "first helix") in three parts: 22 major genes drawn from the business successes (Part 1), four genes drawn from historical failures (Part 2) and a complementary managerial gene (in Part 3). Part 3 then builds the "second helix" by interpreting a number of the major genes into a knowledge base ready for implementation at various companies and organizations.

Part 1 is purely linear thinking: it scans the business *space:* typical business domains of interest and genes from observable or common knowledge, history and analysis. This is an analysis method that we are all accustomed with and which resorts to customary Cartesian problem solving. This is our comfort zone, we wish to expect a stepwise process sequencing the possibilities at hand to choose from, with a user manual that tells us how to proceed. Since a linear thinker wants a list of after all, when sequencing DNA, we start by flattening out its components. Whenever tackling a complicated issue, we try to decompose it into simpler elements, and break down each of them. The results reflect the components and the sum total of them is assumed to cover the whole initial issue at hand, in our case *Apple's DNA content.*

In Part 2, we focus on Apple's blatant old failures, showing that they are at the root of its most recent tremendous success. The chronological sequence of failures scans the dimension of *time.*

From Part 1 and Part 2, a new layer will be built from which to evolve the genes: these cannot be taken as static fixtures.

Hence, Part 3 offers a rather unusual attempt at decoding a firm's DNA. It seeks to activate genes in relation to each other. It builds a new energy. New capacities may emerge that are inscribed in a nonlinear way, not only confounding the past and present, but also modifying the acquired past by building new ones. In doing so, we needed special armory: the power of two special design methodologies. These de-linearize the previous findings and provide an access path to anything that is so uncovered. The DNA becomes a springboard for a firm's future.

One is dedicated to the design of breakthrough innovations and has a unique forcing ability to forge wished properties. It bears the unique capacity to obtain wished results. In other words, it can be applied to transfer the previously found genes into new business realms. The other supports the latter by bringing up a ternary thinking. It will help us to escape from dualistic thinking and is applied to systematizing the ternary thinking for three arguments at the heart of any business:

*Innovating – Branding – Competing*

Part 3 innovates in business thinking by offering an integrated approach to issues. A fitting parallel between Steve Jobs and Leonardo Da Vinci backs our approach and shows how such geniuses depart from the prevalent linear thinking which humanity has been accustomed to so far. Stunning innovation role models illustrate the main stance of this book: the gap with a traditional business thinking, exacerbated by classical business schools. We can say that the way Apple is thinking and operating surely prefigures future thinking and operating ways for a new generation of firms for the coming decades. Will technology blend with art, science with devices and consciousness with action? Will Apple be seen someday soon as the tip of this coming revolution? This is arguable, as Steve Jobs has made decisive breaches in his way of considering computing, devices, design, technology, usage, and, above all, life, that the meaning of these breaches can only be understood when more mature development phases will come of age.

To support Part 3 with the underpinning and methodological rationale, a number of appendices are provided, each bringing in a particular generic tooling apparatus.

This translation is necessary for designing new capacities, and therefore imports those genes into target organizations. It serves as a methodological platform for constructing new cultures.

Several appendices complement the reading and provide, among other additions, the full list of the genes found, a backgrounder for harnessing more genes as time goes on, as well as a comprehensive bibliographical reference.

*"If you want to do something new, do it."*

John Lennon

| Part | Title | Aim and scope |
|---|---|---|
| 1. Business spaces | From insanely successful episodes | Evidencing major cultural gaps that set Apple apart in the business sphere. Discussing a number of salient genes found at Apple in a way that other organizations can import for their own sake. |
| 2. Failure times | From impressive failure passages | Enhancing a number of striking failures which had a major impact on Apple's later successes. Drawing a few genes out of the failures. |
| 3. Quantum spaces | From Apple's genes into transferable knowledge | Accounting for a variety of distinctive features that consolidate the peculiar culture at Apple. |
| Appendices | A collection of methodologies, knowledge and other background material | Supporting the above three parts with generic thinking models. Underpinning a capacity to create genes in a priori any other domains of activity. |

**Table 1.** *Structuring the book from linear to nonlinear thinking*

# Introduction

Even for whoever may not appreciate Apple products (at least, not as much as the authors, which seems possible), Apple Inc. is a fascinating company from a purely business standpoint.

When a company becomes so successful, over such a significant period of time, (which excludes happy coincidences), it is worth analyzing so to draw conclusions which are as general as possible.

Of course, there is no such thing as a silver bullet: success requires effort, risk taking and some people appear as programmed for success, even though they make wrong decisions from time to time, or good decisions based on incorrect reasoning, which defies logic – but probably not business.

Apple, which came so close to disappearing from planet Earth in 1996, has produced ever since such an incredible success that few people may realize that it is the logical sustained endeavor of inner guidance.

Now, on a rocketing track of an approximate $200B annual turnover, $40B profit after taxes and market capitalization on its way to $1 trillion in the near future. On an average stock exchange day, 1% of Apple stock is traded, which is equivalent to the total of exchanges for most European financial places, on the same day. In the past, IBM only achieved a comparable success. IBM market dominance in the 1970s is now something difficult to figure out.

At that time, so-called "IBM watchers" pretended to decipher the giant's strategy from its smallest single moves.

Apple now enjoys the same kind of attention with the notable difference that if only IT industry was concerned in the past with IBM moves, few economic sectors can nowadays safely claim to be unconcerned with Apple moves.

Even though some executives in automobile, banking, watch making industries may issue such claims, these appear to be risky ones, close to the sin of pride, because many companies in recent history (such as RIM and Nokia) have paid a high price for this.

Even Microsoft has undeniably suffered from Apple's success, which amounts to a total reversal of situation, compared with the one existing when Steve Jobs returned to Apple in 1995.

> *"If you know your enemies and know yourself, you will not be imperiled in a hundred battles; if you do not know your enemies but do know yourself, you will win one and lose one; if you do not know your enemies nor yourself, you will be imperiled in every single battle."*
>
> Sun Tzu, *The Art Of War*

Whether you, dear readers, are an Apple customer, a partner or a competitor, or find yourself in a management position, it is of utmost importance to understand Apple's recipe for success.

Through this book, we would like to show that this recipe relies on a small number of guiding principles, contradicting what is usually taught in business schools.

By doing so, we therefore follow Guy Kawasaki (former Apple's Chief Evangelist of the Macintosh period) footsteps, from his iconic title "The Macintosh Way" [KAW 90]. This book (and his author too) is somewhat legendary in the Apple community and beyond, as a rare insider testimony about the radical novelty of early Apple business culture. At that time, however, Apple was the little David fighting against giants, and therefore relying mostly on guerrilla techniques adapted to such situations. Guy Kawasaki's book, although still very insightful, reflects this past situation.

Before passing away, Steve Jobs initiated an Apple University, in order to maintain and propagate Apple's core values internally. The precise content of the courses is likely to remain a secret, but we like to think of our book as an attempt to come closer to it.

Identifying and characterizing what hopefully makes Apple unique, and explain its success, is therefore nothing else than sequencing its DNA.

Each and every company is indeed characterized by a specific DNA, resulting from its history, and key personality aspects of its leaders. May this book open the way to a sort of "genetic engineering" applied to those companies desiring to take advantage of the genes that have been identified therein. And perhaps inspire the founders of new ones.

# From Insanely Successful Episodes

(In Evidence of First-Level Gaps)

# Sequencing the First Segments
# of Apple's DNA

## 1.1. The gene, domain and cultural bias

Every once in a while, a unique individual appears capable of accomplishing changes and, by the same token, showing the rest of us the way to create new paradigms. This seems to happen at the precise moment when mankind needs it. Nikola Tesla was the luminary inventor who harnessed electricity in the first part of the 20th Century. In the arts, John Lennon was an inspiring soul in the time of the Beatles. They acted as accelerators of certain energies. And Apple, fueled by a unique individual, was the company that helped carry technology to new computing and entertainment paradigms.

All these exceptional individuals share a singular way of thinking about things. Nikola Tesla tested his amazingly complicated apparatus mentally until he found functional proof, whereas John Lennon coined sentences that still propagate around the world, each with an enhanced thinking signature, free of linear structure. Where does such an ability come from? What is the DNA sequence of that nonlinear thinking? Where are the genes which account for a sustained capacity in a given domain? Do we all share them within ourselves? How do we locate and possibly activate them?

Can science fiction come to the rescue? If we imagine these genes as time capsules that are already available – but which we normally find ourselves unable to open – it would perhaps seem appropriate to iconize them with a pictured cryptic diagram. These would be the application icons to operate. The following chapters feature a little icon to remember this possibility within ourselves. Not as fancy as those on your iPhone, but simply a handy recalling factor. These are your time capsules available for launching.

To pinpoint these genes, we will begin by listing a number of key domains of concern which often puzzle entrepreneurs. These are subject matters for debate in academic circles and they are often bound to cultural prejudices. What is it that distinguishes Silicon Valley from other regions of the globe, if not a radically different ambient culture? We tend to view business culture as a frequency, where each of us resonates to some of these frequencies and much less to others.

Cultural biases are formed throughout our formative years and mature into *fixations*, mental constructs inhibiting change. Some are good or even necessary, because they ensure we hold on to something valuable. For instance, acquired skills usually lead to fixation. Or they can be detrimental to change and to thinking outside the box – i.e. breaking the rules – by stopping a mental dynamic for learning or improving something. We always tend to create fixations, but we lack the mechanism to know when to overlay them and when to not. The point is this: when a company outrightly breaks fixations, it may venture into a golden unknown or risk its future. Where do we draw the line?

From a given domain of business relevance (e.g. "competition" in the first column), Table 1.1 establishes that line in the form of one or more questions to ask (the middle column) as a potential breaking axis. These questions are meant to trigger progress, which involves revisiting the way in which we consider a given relevance domain. Finally, from these questions we draw one core issue ready to be debated by antagonizing "the Apple way" and "the business school way".

## 1.2. Nine DNA segments of rare importance

This book bases its findings on the biological metaphor of DNA that every living organism is bound to sustain life. Sustainability is both the aim and the capability that a living entity strives to ensure. Sustainability is the only core determination that underpins all others. It is a difficult subject matter, in good part not well understood and there are few methods for making it a reality, be it at a company, nation or planet level [MAS 15a, MAS 15b]. Despite a great amount of work in the sustainability domain, there is no such science of sustainability yet.

As pointed out by Diamond [DIA 05], some past civilizations followed a path which lead to their collapse (Mayan civilization, Easter Island society, etc.). This cannot be designated as a collective suicide: societies never consciously commit suicide, but they may take disastrous decisions, which produce the same effect. The same analysis can be applied at a company or individual level.

Recognizing sustainability as the primary objective, for any organization, at any level of size or complexity, is not enough: the real question is how to achieve this goal.

In this simple recognition of the living imperative, nine domains of consideration pop up together that are usually considered independently in the business spheres, taught separately by respective experts and executed in distinct branches or services. They are actually connected to each other, and express an even simpler global concept:

*How can a striving firm be made sustainable?*

Let us now scan each of the nine core issues in Table 1.1.

| | Key business issues | The associated fundamental, often hidden, questions to consider | Traditional thinking versus Apple approach |
|---|---|---|---|
| *it* | *Typical issues that CEOs consider (and make them so busy)* | *This is not the traditional way to think about the domains of interest* | *Reformulating the domain to reveal inner impact* |
| *1* | Uncertainty | *Where is risk? Where is opportunity? (not what, but where)* | Risk Taking |
| 2 | Products | *Which products to offer and those to not offer? (saying 'no' before a 'yes') Form of function? Where's the optimum trade-off?* | Product design |
| *3* | Markets | *Does the market really know about tomorrow?* | Market studies |
| 4 | Competition | *Where is competition? Where it is not? (not what, but where)* | Giving up some fights |
| 5 | Leadership | *Are markets solid things or just alterable identities?* | Entering new markets |
| 6 | Skills and talents | *What's in a failure: a test or a lesson? An exit or a ticket to success?* | Apple, the Learning Company |
| 7 | R&D | *Can R&D be decoupled from cost? Is innovation coupled to R&D?* | On R&D |
| 8 | External growth | *Is success correlated market share? Where's value?* | On company acquisition |
| 9 | Software versus Hardware | *Is software development manageable? How differently?* | Managing Software development |

**Table 1.1.** *In free market economies, firms face eternal issues to consider. Exploring their core subsets reveals hidden issues to bring into consideration*

# 2

# On Risk Taking

## 2.1. Where is the gap?

Risk or reward? Danger lurks not only within the business route but also within opportunities. Why do we retain such a dualistic view for a single term? After all, "venture capitalism" originates from the latin *adventura* (literally "toward the venture, the possibilities"). But it was then renamed as *risk capital*!

### 2.1.1. *Business school*

Beyond the official presentations trying to portray how innovative the organization is, the sad and sordid reality is that every manager is in fact, at a personal level at least, allergic to risk, for the simple reason that an elementary cost/benefit analysis quickly convinces him that risk taking does not pay off, in terms of career development.

Moreover, traditional business school teaching puts so much emphasis on risk analysis that cautiousness easily turns into risk aversion.

Even in cases where the innovative forces of the company manage to come up with a promising new product, it is frequently rejected, based on the idea that a new product could sabotage the existing products, which characterize an organization perceiving its own innovation (and innovators) as a threat.

In traditional sectors, characterized by slow innovation, managers may never, or very seldom in an entire career, forced to decide on a major disruptive innovation. The bulk of innovation happens through small, incremental, low risk and low cost improvements.

However, even in those sectors, there always comes a time when the digital era is about to overthrow everything:

– in the automobile industry: the connected electric car, possibly driverless in the future, if socially accepted;

– in the media industry used to sell newspapers and magazines: the electronic distribution of content;

– etc.

Managers wired with traditional MBA thinking often find themselves unable to deal with such revolutions, and will always find good reasons to stay away from them and even shield themselves from it with *a priori* arguments and solid justifications.

But in the post-modern digital age, disregarding such revolutions is equivalent to suicide.

Most traditional managers only manage one thing: their career. They condemn to death the companies they work for, yet do not care much because their own survival instinct will tell them when to jump out of the boat before it sinks. A reptilian brain is always on the watch, quick to escape through fire the door.

### 2.1.2. *Apple*

Apple has managed to introduce several products, which, as its co-founder Steve Jobs said, are of the "*once in a lifetime*" category: the Mac, the iPod, the iPhone and the iPad. And more recently, under his successor Tim Cook, the Apple watch.

It is easy to forget that these did not fit within any existing known product category, and initially created strong negative reactions.

> *The nature of the personal computer is simply not fully understood by companies like Apple (or anyone else for that matter). Apple makes the arrogant assumption of thinking that it knows what you want and need. It, unfortunately, leaves the "why" out of the equation – as in "why would I want this?" The Macintosh uses an experimental pointing device called a "mouse". There is no evidence that people want to use these things.*

San Francisco Examiner, John C. Dvorak, 19 Feb. 1984

Apple innovated in aspects other than pure technology: one of the key iTunes innovative features was the possibility to buy songs individually. A "whole product" (according to the definition of marketing academic Rogers [ROG 83]) is more than the original tangible product; it must include everything the customer needs and wants for using the product comfortably and with a positive experience.

## 2.2. Amplifying the gap and progressing

Many companies are afraid of sabotaging themselves with their own products. This is a classical topic in business school lectures. It has produced an obstacle of fear for decision makers. A terrible consequence is the resulting brake put on innovations. Innovating involves venturing into the unknown; it is not about dealing with uncertainty. If you don't open up to innovation, competitors will and could steal the market from your own hands.

Uncertainty and the unknown is widely observed as confusing in post-modern business and this has devastating consequences. First, what is uncertain boils down to probabilities, is amenable to some causal reasoning and there are many applied mathematical techniques available to cope with it. Risk analysis is then processed as computing the probability of the occurrence of an event or scenario, etc.

*"To boldly go where no man has gone before"* was the evolved title sequence of most *Star Trek* science fiction episodes. Indeed, innovating radically consists in venturing where no one has gone before: going into the unknown, not quite the uncertain; no well-formed statistics have been received, and the customer may not have noticed any path going "somewhere there". Actually, when you really, honestly innovate, you do not know where you are headed. Accepting this fact is a prerequisite to reap the benefits of innovating. Hence, you will inevitably encounter failures on

your way (Part 2 will detail a reasonable number of Apple's failures). The point is this, wherever you go, you must know why. Be traceable and transparent to yourself, following a constructive approach, detecting the "moments of innovation", i.e. the very step where you are branching into a new direction which bears fruits.

Do not confuse the risk that comes from a low probability of success and the opportunity that arises from following a dark path. If you search for your lost glasses under the lamppost, you can compute the probability of (not) finding them. You want light, and light has already given the answer to your question. You may intensify the light and search a bit further down on the sidewalk, but are you searching in the right direction?

The "fear quotient" is a natural ingredient in human personality. But pure innovation players have no such fear. They have an inner light lighting the obscure path they're treading against all odds. They see beyond obstacles and risk analysis is not their daily tool for calculating their next step. They use a positive approach which seems to be their fuel. And it helps them when jumping into regions which have not been lighted by anybody yet. They think using their acquired genes (of the ancestors companies and business practices) and create new ones.

We know of only one framework which is exactly designed to systematically tackle the unknown. C-K theory form *Ecole des Mines ParisTech* explains why and we use Appendix 4 to introduce it. Furthermore, it provides all the design properties mentioned above: it is constructive, traceable, and accounts for the "Eureka moments" which intensely sign off the unique moments when something "clicks" before us. We have used it at length for understanding Leonardo Da Vinci deeper, as well as artists as René Magritte Salvador Dali, and in new ways.

Free yourself from the probability/predisposition way and enter the free path to the unknown: there lie the breakthroughs that will change the world. Neurologists may say that this is equivalent to opening up the possibilities of the right hemisphere of the brain, since the left one is believed to measure uncertainty. This is the stunning "*Stay Hungry. Stay Foolish*" motto delivered at the end of Steve Jobs' address at Stanford University in 2005. In other terms: "*Dare to go where nobody has gone before*".

A risk-oriented attitude is grounded on fear. And the opposite is certainly not ignoring risk! It is opening roads in the dark. This is genuine "craziness", in terms of the corresponding attitude that stands apart from the mainstream. But this is the way to become a master of your own future. The individuals who follow this thread participate in their own creation. Why fear what you contribute to create? Why fear if you create the ways to design desired futures? C-K theory can dramatically help in this future design field [COR 13]. It's a way to learn to not be a victim of competition or of the mainstream, to escape the duality that reigns in competitive markets[1]. This liquidates what you owe as third (competitors, partners, etc.) references and you free yourself from any related accounting. You become the author of a new "truth".

Innovation comes from within before becoming an outside artifact, so express your truth and strive. No other player is meant to dictate what you have inside. When Jobs said "*I have at least another 4 to 5 products in my stomach*" during the 2000s, he was surely referring to that inner drive that authors fresh new creations, not those of others, an ability to really create entire new worlds and which requires to be in a sense "unfaithful" to obsolete arrangements.

For instance, there are industrial standard ways of doing things, the ways we've been using so far. When Apple abandoned the CD reader in MacBooks, or added a Thunderbolt port, or removed all ports but the Thunderbolt on MacBook Airs, what was this, if not leaving current practice behind (however still possible via a device) and opening new ones that bear new performance for the user? They are not procedures, but conscious moves beyond procedures! They express a deliberate intention, which is to be sensed for the user side. And for Apple, it means the breaking of a silent contract with industry. The way of the leader is always to set ourselves as an example and not to control others! Business schools have here a case study to disseminate.

However, this also means quitting a path which was entered some time ago (the Innovation Capability Maturity Model details this mechanism, see [COR 15]).

In his book *The Macintosh Way* [KAW 90], Guy Kawasaki, a marketing member of the historical core team, outlines one aspect of Steve Jobs' personality, for which he uses the term "Chutzpah".

This difficult to translate word comes from Hebrew. Standard translations include audacity, insolence, impudence, gall, brazen nerve, effrontery, incredible

---

1 Blue Ocean strategy [KIM 05] was instrumental in showing us how to value strategic market spaces that turn their back to competition: not focusing on costs and margins, but on the couple (innovation, value). We have used it in innumerable situations and found it an irreplaceable tool for dealing with value. However, it cannot help to *design* a solution and this is where C-K theory comes into play.

guts, presumption and even arrogance. Kawasaki gives several examples of Chutzpah[2]:

> *"Calling up tech support to report a bug on pirated software."*

or:

> *"Steve is off the scale when it comes to Chutzpah. He used a slide in the 1985 shareholders meeting showing a mock-up of the Wall Street Journal with headline 'Apple proposes Detente with IBM'."*

**Figure 2.1.** *Jobs triggers chutzpah by reversing dominance in a mocked leading newspaper in the eighties*

He also adds:

> *"The great thing about Chutzpah is that it inspires people to exceed their capabilities. Steve wanted to defeat IBM, not "achieve 18 percent market share". Epic battles are not measured in market share percentage points, and people will fight to the death if they are led by a guy with Chutzpah."*

---

2 "Bill Gates, accused by Jobs of ripping off the Apple interface for Windows, replied: 'Well, Steve, I think there's more than one way of looking at it. I think it's more like we both had this rich neighbor named Xerox and I broke into his house to steal the TV set only to find that you had already stolen it'. *I think that's called 'chutzpah'.* Cited by Prof. Tom Wilson, http://www.informationr.net/ir/reviews/revs156.html (as of 2004).

A well argued and solidly justified position! When we left IBM in California in the year 1981, our San Jose Research Laboratory immediately ordered 240 IBM personal computers upon its announcement on August 12, 1981. Shortly after, we were working at IBM La Gaude Study and Research Center near Nice in France: they timidly ordered two of them and locked them in a room! Were these little PCs too intimidating for the monster mainframes of the time?

Remember: Chutzpah is the trigger which unbolts the wheels of fixation.

## 2.3. The genes

In this particular case, we have an Apple gene directly derived from Steve Jobs' DNA. No doubt this gene is still present in Apple's DNA.

---

Gene **AAPL001 – Accept risk, turn it into opportunity**

*If you do not accept risk, then keep away from any business.*

Gene **AAPL002 – Have Chuztpah.**

*Excellence in management requires Chutzpah.*

---

# 3

---

# Product Design

---

## 3.1. Where is the gap?

You said product? Who designs products? Designers and developers, of course. And they are good at it, since they do it all the time. So, why bother?

### 3.1.1. *Business school*

Product design: it is an engineering discipline, out of the scope of a good manager.

Product definition: the marketing defines the products to be developed, the technical teams execute this vision.

Period. And then...

About your catalog: your product catalog will obey the 80-20 rule. Accept this by balancing your earnings.

On packing with functionality: as competition shrinks your market share, add value with more functionality.

### 3.1.2. *Apple*

Products must be "insanely great", which implies a number of choices, not all technical in the usual sense, including form and function. Extreme care is taken to any of them, whether resulting in a visible result or not. Design is iterated on as many prototypes as needed to feel convinced at the end that the best choices have been made, irrespective of costs and delays. The top-level manager is involved and committed in this process. There is no place for "good enough" products.

To heck with the 80-20 rule. Get rid of the useless part. Almost everything should be essential. The 80-20 rationale view is a common tolerance view on lesser quality. You do not educate markets. You stay in the midst of other's complacencies. An 80-80 rule, perhaps should be your close win. Perfection in what you do.

## 3.2. Amplifying the gap and progressing

Raymond Loewy published the famous book *Ugliness Sells Itself Badly* in 1953. Nobody would challenge this statement. Yet, here we have evidence which is, strangely enough, systematically forgotten, at a time when companies desperately strive for the smallest selling point.

Anyone can recognize that Apple products are beautiful, or "*insanely great*". Hewlett Packard's CEO Meg Whitman declares speaking about the PC market:

> "*The whole market has moved to something that is more beautiful. Apple taught us that design really matters.*"

However, instead of humbly recognizing that a lot remains to be done to sustain comparison with Apple, she immediately added:

> "*I think we've made a lot of progress.*"

A typical self-satisfactory CEO statement, and a totally unproductive one.

Jony Ives' role and position at Apple does not deserve a lengthy discussion. Granting a designer such a prominent position in an organization is something unheard of outside of the fashion business.

Some argue that Apple's obsession for the form factor sometimes goes as far as being detrimental to function. For example, they complain that they would prefer an iPhone with a larger battery, instead of thickness reduction.

Apple tends to adopt a minimalist, Zen-spirit approach: "*more*" is not necessarily better, and where competitors struggle to enrich the spec sheet, Apple simplifies and strips down to the essential.

Whereas most designers are proud of the list of functionality they have managed to implement, the Apple designer is proud of those he has eliminated.

In its commercials, Apple highlights user experience, and never pure technical specifications ("spec sheet"). There is more: user experience starts from the moment the customer unpacks the products, by holding and looking at the pack. Jony Ives' recent new assignment extends user experience even further to "customer experience": customer satisfaction must be the objective, whether the customer interacts with an Apple product, an Apple Website or a physical Apple Store.

In order to decide whether a given functionality must be present in the product or not, Apple performs a detailed analysis of the different interaction contexts (the "use cases").

Many companies consider that it is best to let the market decide between possible choices. Following a "*throw against the wall and see if it sticks*" strategy, they disperse their efforts into a multitude of product lines. This is typical of Samsung's strategy in the smartphone business.

Apple follows this unique path, even though some competitors may begin to realize they would do well in borrowing from it.

Apple products are easy to use, so easy that the user manual is kept down to the bare minimum. They rely on choices which appear obvious, yet ones nobody thought to use before.

Apple competitors probably also have ergonomists, and there is no reason to believe that they are stupid. The difference is that, at Apple, their opinion is considered as valuable, and taken into account, at the right time.

Steve Jobs insisted on the fact that he was taking more pride in what he rejected than in what he accepted:

> "*I'm as proud of many of the things we haven't done as the things we have done. Innovation is saying no to a thousand things.*"

Too often, the designer is requested to incorporate a long list of features, which leads to compromise and ineffective design choices.

Apple will not hesitate to eliminate features which it considers as heritage from the past (diskettes drive, CD/DVD drives more recently, even USB ports even recently on the Mac Air). At first, strong dissatisfaction reactions can be heard, but rather quickly the Apple choice is accepted and propagates to competitors products. The issue here is, therefore, to be the first who is courageous enough to *say no*.

Apple's strategy is similar to the one used by Nature: in living organisms, organs and functions occupy the volume they need, given the advantage they bring in competition for life or reproduction – nothing more, nothing less.

Apple avoids duplicating, like Nature. Whenever Nature duplicates, there is a good reason behind: safety redundancy (lungs and kidneys), or new functionality (two eyes bring stereoscopic vision and two ears bring sound spatial information).

If, for some reason, for example a change in the environment, a function is no longer needed, it simply disappears.

This selectivity, combined with the compactness of Apple design solutions, sparing both material and energy, is the true ecological way of designing products, following Nature's lessons.

In traditional (often vertically organized) organizations, the company history and the delicate balance resulting from power struggles at the top lead to an implicit hierarchy between functions, valuing some opinions more than others, simply depending on what function in the company executives come from. A *de facto* situation which preempts products-market preferences independently of …the market.

### 3.2.1. *On packing with functionality*

Keep it simple and focus on *coherence*, since the value of the product is not the sum of the value of the functionality. And the value of the whole catalog is not the sum of values of the products that compose it.

Remember Nokia's Communicator? The first smartphone equipped with Windows, packing a ton of functions. The result: big, heavy, slower and slower operations as garbage collection was inefficient. Or the first HTC smartphones.

Ken Segall, the former agency creative director for NeXT and Apple, is the guy who put the 'i' in iPad. He explained why simplicity is the secret of Apple's success in *Insanely Simple* [SEG 13]:

> *"To Steve Jobs, simplicity wasn't just a design principle. It was a religion and a weapon. The obsession with simplicity is what separates Apple from other technology companies. It's what helped Apple recover from near-death in 1997 to become the most valuable company on Earth in 2011, and guides the way Apple is organized, how it designs products, and how it connects with customers. It's by crushing the forces of complexity that the company remains on its stellar trajectory."*

Complexity requires simplicity. Complications (resulting from the staking of more functions) distract the user, who then loses the perception of "one product".

In product design, the ergonomist is no less important than the engineer. His role is to bring that final cosmetic touch of "beauty" on the product after it is designed. When it comes to the product, no idea and no people profile are to be disregarded without further examination.

We always like to point out for our children that if Steve Jobs did not have the strange idea to follow calligraphy training courses at an early age, the beautiful fonts which came together with the original Mac would have never appeared so early in computer history.

And that is the "connecting dots" metaphor of Steve Jobs in his famous Stanford speech:

> *"You can't connect the dots looking forward; you can only connect them looking backwards. So you have to trust that the dots will somehow connect in your future. You have to trust in something – your gut, destiny, life, karma, whatever. Because believing that the dots will connect down the road will give you the confidence to follow your heart even when it leads you off the well-worn path; and that will make all the difference."*

Steve Jobs, Stanford Speech, June 12, 2005

---

Gene **AAPL003 – Product is more than product.**
  *The design team's objective is to come up with an "insanely great" product.*

Gene **AAPL004 – Turn essentials inside out.**
  *Removing what is unnecessary is more valuable than blindly stacking functionality.*

Gene **AAPL005 – Product existence is by using it.**

*Enhancing customer experience rather than the spec. sheet.*

Gene **AAPL006 – Always keep the end in sight.**

*Polarize all developments by working toward an aim.*

Gene **AAPL007 – Be your own judge.**

*The best approach to come up with an "insanely great" product for designers is to realize the product they would have liked to buy.*

# Market Studies

## 4.1. Where is the gap?

*"Is there a market?"*, *"how big is the market?"* is a startup existence mantra that resonates like the sword of Damocles. When identifying a demand craze, what are the right questions to ask? The art of approaching the market is as important as a hopeful traction it may have on all competitors.

### 4.1.1. *Business school*

Subcontract costly market studies.

Market analysis mantra: exercise your marketing stamina by analyzing markets before entering them.

Segment the company offering accordingly, making sure that the maximum coverage of identified needs is achieved. You should envisage covering your market segments to the point of saturation.

Oh! And use the market studies to define the price tag.

Exploit a concept.

### 4.1.2. *Apple*

Postulate: customers don't anticipate what technology can do. Even if they sometimes could.

**Figure 4.1.** *Energy roots access, which roots... the rest of it (source: http://angkor.co/photo/basic-human-needs-added-two-more-wifi-battery)*

Apple shows no interest in traditional detailed market analysis, and only considers global market size and product type renewal rhythm.

Remain focused. Concentrate on Premium offering, leave the rest to the competitors, which will fight to the death in a race to the bottom.

Reinvent an existing concept. Make the best product.

### 4.2. Amplifying the gap and progressing

Saturation-driven companies lose their DNA: they want to be hegemonic, hence sacrifice part of their soul to "external" aspirations.

Apple's genetics lies in striking unexpected products seemingly out of the blue. As long as this is maintained, they remain aligned with their root gene.

Certainly, considering that the competitive race may not be a problem – as long as the product is attractive enough – requires courage and absence of fear. It is fear that calls for piling up reports. After all, aren't market studies sort of reports? Guess where do reports end up, usually? Using a report is like using snapshot photography to capture full high speed motion. The shielding from studies analyzing markets isn't a protection for any market warrior.

Courage is often assimilated to risk. And the expectation of risk entails fear. Locking the company in a deadly treadmill isn't any entrepreneurs wish.

Take a different view. Shift your angle.

You can't do everything: do one thing and do it well. Even if this means turning your back on competition.

Listening to others will certainly inform you, in the same way as listening to all radio or TV channels will not inform you any more (let alone any better) – you get a lot of noise. You even mime noise. And this becomes costly to get rid of. The more you listen to the noises, the more you tend to add features to your products. They become heavy and unsound at best, irrelevant at worst. You end up being a me-too clone.

The best product doesn't mean the most complicated, the richest in features, or the most technologically advanced. Marketing practice has shown this for a long time. "Best" means a combination of product quality, timing and irresistible appeal. Market analysis may have shown that there is "no visible market" or "no market traction", but sex appeal triggers the "boom".

Begin by simplifying product range down to the minimum. This will bear the virtue to focus on design effort; it will maximize economies of scale; and, by the way, it will simplify logistics too.

Now, the question is how do you do this? First, it's by saying "no" to everything which isn't essential. In this way, you begin to focus on the kernel axis that carries only the key aspects. An example is the long list of functions for future products: you have got to rank them and set things to the top for the most important ones. Customers may not help much here: they just can't extract the quintessence of the products they're using, they see the variety, they like it, and that just comfort them. You're better off relying on deep intuition.

Practice lateral thinking. See the rabbit in the chest full of nuts. Can you see a portable office in a telephone? iPhone! Can you see a downloadable song in a music disk? iTunes! By authoring a new category of products aligned with latent demand, and positioning it to the top, you'll let many others enter the game, but at lower positions, where the fight is the fiercest.

In Spring 2011, soon after the iPhone and the iPad introduction generated hysteria, competitors announced "soon to come" vaporware products. It took time to see the promise of serious competition to control market share, but they never reached profits share.

---

Gene **AAPL008 – Impose strategic rhythm to markets.**

*Do not become a "me-too" supplier. Anything you launch should be strategic.*

Gene **AAPL009 – Aim for the top.**

*By thinking from the top, you let others consolidate your basis – from below.*

---

# Giving up Some Fights

## 5.1. The chasm

Duality is our legacy. Battles always have two camps. One must win and the other loses. One will negotiate and the others adapt. It is written so in our genes' legacy. We say *"survival of the fittest"* and accept the penalty for lack of contest, supremacy and luck.

### 5.1.1. *Business school*

We can try to escape from an inferior business situation by acquiring a competitor, or increasing budgets.

Engaging in head-on combat or giving up the fight forever are the only two alternatives.

### 5.1.2. *Apple*

When Steve Jobs returned to Apple, his very first decisions were focused on one single objective: concentrate all company resources on a limited number of projects and products, and abolish all the others. This included even the Newton, or the QuickTake camera, etc.

The condition of Apple by then admittedly left him with no other option. However, even with the virtually unlimited resources it now can mobilize, Apple can adopt an unusually modest approach in some business categories.

## 5.2. Amplifying the gap and progressing

> *"To win one hundred victories in one hundred battles is not the acme of skill. To subdue the enemy without fighting is the acme of skill."*
>
> Sun Tzu, *The Art Of War*

Even if Apple did not remain totally inactive, with its own offering (iWorks), the iWorks suite has clearly never been a priority, and remained largely unchanged over a long period (except recently, on the occasion of a move toward a Cloud offering). When Oracle decided at one point in time to be involved in Open Office (which resulted in the Libre Office fork), this could have been a good opportunity for Apple to jump in this boat, but they did not (Oracle finally gave up on Open Office in 2011).

Office suites, for example, still remain the killer application in the business world, and Microsoft long enjoyed an undisputed dominant position in this market. But eventually, the time has come in favor of Apple. What was a major weakness in Apple's offering in 1997 is no longer a major concern, because PCs now are used for a myriad of other things than office suites, and a number of alternatives to Microsoft Office now exist, including the free Libre Office Suite.

Microsoft never ceased proposing a Mac version to its Office suite (although without extreme enthusiasm...) and recently came to the conclusion that it could no longer ignore the iOS market share. Accordingly, it decided to develop iOS versions of its MS Office suite.

In a subtle way, the Sun Tzu quote applies well to this case and Apple is on its way to winning, without having had any head-on fighting.

In the same line of thought, when Steve Jobs presented the iPod with iTunes, the announcement was then perceived as a minor and insignificant move, failing to bring any suitable answer to Apple's major weakness on the PC market (which, by the way, was the only one on which Apple was present at that time).

A lengthy explanation is not required. Hindsight clarifies what the grand design behind this brilliant move was: repositioning Apple on markets with considerably more potential than that of the PC alone, and paving the way for a "post PC" era, which is now putting Microsoft into trouble.

OK, being as smart as Steve Jobs cannot be that easy. However, the above examples show that battles in which a wise general refuses to engage exist. Why so? Because chances of success are too small.

In such a situation, shifting to another – widely unexpected – battlefield may be far more clever. An operations room that yields plenty of time to gain strong positions, before competitors, could help us understand what is the hell going on out there.

Alas, lots of companies, especially the ones which can afford the muscled up strategy, do privilege frontal assault. They routinely use their financial resources to regain a lost advantage. When Microsoft saw trouble on the cell phone market acquired a bundle of companies at an extremely high price. Skype was acquired at $8.5B in 2011. Microsoft paid about $1,000 for every Skype customer, whereas, on average, those customers were worth a profit of about $30 each. Four years later, the business justification still appears questionable.

Arguably, the more a company succeeds in something, the more it is tempted to stick to it and never depart from. Perhaps the most striking example is the absolutely huge Office plus Windows installed everywhere, at a time when consumers – and more and more enterprises – were centering their daily life on mobile applications. This seems to oppose persistence (another gene we spotted), but what is orthodox persistence against the waves of the future? Big ruptures have to be taken into consideration and pondered before it is too late. For the way out must be paralleled with doing something else. As PCs took over the user world from mainframes in the 1980s, mobile computing is taking over PCs in the 2010s. Shifting battlegrounds from PC software and platforms was long overdue for Microsoft. But, the genetics of the company has not been the inventing new markets – never. Perhaps, it will be able to capitalize on a "new mature" market someday by redoing Bill Gates's coup for IBM's DOS operating system? But, PCs-as-a-commodity have lost their value and troubled waters loom; will PCs be soon free to use?

When the leveraging point is lost, value goes away and it means it is time to employ divergent thinking, not convergent: to think of alternative routes in a radical way, e.g. to connect unexpected things to what we know or do best. For instance, socially networked ways of working. The criterion that measures the creativity is "variety", as opposed to "consistency". There must be ways to harness the vast knowledge base that Microsoft has nurtured with Office and Windows series and redirect it to new things. This requires generating variability (*"whether convergent or divergent products result depends upon the way in which this thinking power is applied: to produce more of the same, or to generate novelty"* [CRO 15b]) or stagnation, then regression will ensue.

Given its financial resources, Apple could virtually buy any company on the planet. Only competitive market authorities and regulators could possibly impose limits, in some cases.

For any other MBA-wired manager, the obvious strategy to follow would be to engage a massive acquisition policy, rather than remain seated on this huge pile of cash.

But, this is not in line with Apple's DNA.

Apple's talent to select the fights which deserve to be fought can also be related to this famous Steve Jobs quote:

> *"There's an old Wayne Gretzky quote that I love. 'I skate to where the puck is going to be, not where it has been.' And we've always tried to do that at Apple. Since the very very beginning. And we always will."*

Steve Jobs, Macworld Conference and Expo in Jan. 2007

---

Gene **AAPL010 – Anticipate.**

> *A lower position can no longer be overcome through frontal assault on the same battleground, rather by skating where the puck is going to be.*

Gene **AAPL011 – Select your fights.**

> *This strategy requires patience, as the puck may move slowly.*

---

# Entering New Markets

## 6.1. The chasm

The *way* to enter new markets reveals the style of leadership to come for the products at stake.

First mover or second mover? Advantages versus disadvantages. The one who moves ahead first on new markets takes all the burden. The price to pay for maximum freedom and, later, dominance. Followers need to differentiate themselves, or alternatively accept to be perceived as "me-too" players. How do we mitigate a dilemma?

### 6.1.1. *Business school*

Keep your objectives. Manage by objectives (external to people).

Traditional thinking commands a simple line of action. First, you cannot refuse a tempting opportunity, because you have weighed up the attainable volumes. Second, entering new markets is so risky that this move should, therefore, only be performed gradually, taking advantage of similarities with existing products/markets. Or by acquiring external companies, and thus capturing the corresponding market share.

So, reassure your markets by saying what is next. What is going to be next? What could be next and is not yet.

Minimizing surprise effect to comforting markets, that is minimizing risks. After all, do markets not abhor two things above all: vacuum and risk?

### 6.1.2. *Apple*

> *"We're always thinking about new markets we could enter, but it's only by saying no that you can concentrate on the things that are really important."*

Steve Jobs, *Business-Week*, Oct. 12, 2004

Apple demonstrated a keen capacity to penetrate markets in which it had none or almost no experience at all.

Ensure quality first for great products. A gene for success is in the product (the source).

A market is the exteriorization of the source. Get back to the source, there is no substitute.

### 6.2. Amplifying the gap and progressing

So, to return again Apple entering other unexpected markets. For instance, what about the automobile market? But look again, the automobile can be considered as a special instance of a mobile equipment. That mobile could be versatile enough to be used, at will, perhaps as an office, and not solely as a transportation mean for leisure or business purpose. And it may not even require a driver!

Various speculations can be made on how Apple may in the future combine, in a radically new way, existing products categories. Best exemple is Steve Jobs, in his famous 2007 presentation, announcing *"three revolutionary devices"*: a wide screen iPod, a mobile Phone, and an internet communicator… which ultimately turned out to be a single device: the iPhone.

Is this future or present? When do we use the future tense and the present tense? Innovating is about thinking now what others will see tomorrow. So, why do we use the future tense? To resolve the gap, which is a source of unresolvable anxiety for markets, move the camera out of sight: do not talk about your future products. Second, you do not know the exact path to market: timing and other issues always impede the linear approach. Think of the *"infinite loops"* announcements by companies (perhaps Microsoft?) and remove the need to have to later argument about changes in strategy.

There is arguably a stock of rationale in this. First, your energy is limited. Keep your energy like a monk does. Do you want to fragment it by managing the response to your visions of the future? This would lead you entertaining a whole discussion with ever would-be customers.

In a nutshell, it is not the objective that is meaningful, it is the end. Leonardo Da Vinci: *"always keep the end in sight"*.

The promising market potential of good ideas may frequently be ruined by poor timing.

When innovating, keeping objectives fixed and stable is, by definition, impossible. But not having the end in sight is behaving like a weather vane. The end becomes your focus: it keeps you tight and safe against (trade, tempting directions, etc.) winds. It may well be that the target remains out of reach; still, it provides a compass for navigating your innovation.

Project management is completely overhauled when you do innovation. You cannot simply manage by objectives since you do not know them yet. *A priori* given objectives reveal obstacles which you may want to avoid. The management purpose is to create the conditions for staff to move with force (internalized for people). Add resilience to your vision and do not confuse resilience with sustainability.

Under the dissolving agency of digital age technologies, categories blur nowadays, and new groups are formed from old divisions, which were not previously seen as approved and controlled nomenclatures.

We commonly tend to take the existing classifications for granted. But, what about the traditional taxi business at an age when self-driving cars come to the road in numbers? It is not Netscape that came to dominate a rejuvenated music business, but it was Netscape that breached the wall of closed music listening for the teenagers once for all in the 1990s. The price to pay was huge both for the sustainability of Netscape and some young, heavy music listeners (or, better, their parents). But, the damage caused to the traditional music business ecosystem was irreversible. If you reinvent, not the automobile, but personal transportation, by dematerializing ownership of cars and build applications operated from platforms, then you instantaneously own the usufruct of all the cars in the world by federating a huge ecosystem of players, without having to pay anything for their maintenance, minus the usage.

Apple's past track record of innovating shows that no product category can be immune to alteration, therefore excluded from innovation strategies. Yet, the only requirement may be that the new target market must be strategically expressed in B\$, or better in tens of B\$, for one chief reason: as it happened in oil business, then in pharmaceutics long ago, this is now the elementary accounting unit for Apple.

> Gene **AAPL012 – See the new in the old.**
>
> *A new category is formed out of blurring the divisions between old ones.*

# Apple, the Learning Company

## 7.1. The chasm

You know your core business. You know what you know and you also know what you do not know (which perhaps you should not know either). Your experience guides you. Enough knowledge is enough: concentrating on what you do best is always your safest net for the future.

Do the dynamics of success make companies fall asleep after a while? After the start-up phase, it is said that growth must happen to succeed and reap the benefits of initial investments. Success in one domain attracts success, but the downside of it is that you tend to confine yourself to the same narrow domain, again and again. Does a looming fate of being successful blind us again to the hidden learning needed to perform?

### 7.1.1. *Business school*

The traditional school of thought is to put emphasis on how to avoid making any mistakes and failures. This conservative attitude lends to risk aversion, at all levels of management.

Which attitudes tend to develop a company culture hostile to innovations, especially disruptive ones?

### 7.1.2. *Apple*

> *"I have learned from my mistakes, and I am sure I can repeat them exactly."*

Peter Cook

> *"I'm convinced that about half of what separates successful entrepreneurs from the non-successful ones is pure perseverance."*

Steve Jobs

In the Apple way of managing a company, the company keeps the agility of a start up, whatever its size. So, you can still reinvent yourself.

Think (and do) something different.

Start-up genes are peculiar: focused on rebirth. Those of grown-ups are even more focused on steady-state governance: they fossilize little by little irrevocably. Where is the biggest gain? The gain is not only quantitative, but it is also qualitative.

Break the syllogism:

1) success attracts success;

2) you already succeed at something;

3) therefore, do more of that something.

For example, Kodak Digital Corp. (successful minis were found sitting in between two big segments attacking them), and perhaps, Microsoft's Windows and Office to some extent.

Detach yourself from the present conditions, because your customers are tied in and cannot extract themselves.

Be bold (and wise) enough to escape from the routine of success rut, and think about something else. The best time is *"the moment you begin to feel some perceivable comfort"*. Get out of the rut then: it is a looming basket of pitfall.

Microsoft dwelled in Windows and Office ruts for a long time, despite the huge returns from its dominant market share. A 2015 Windows 10 subsumes an invisible Windows 9, so to mark exiting the rut and send the corresponding marketing message.

Be a highly innovative company, prepared to take huge bets and risks. Accept failure as part of company culture. For every lesson that can be learned from failures, take into account its messages for the future. Sometimes, this will be many years later, and under a totally different approach. What failure tells us is that it is a bitter golden nugget you have paid for and others have possibly not. It is all yours, ready for transmutation into successes.

## 7.2. Amplifying the gap and progressing

> *"I'll be back."*
>
> *The Terminator* (1984)

Did Apple give up the computer market after the Lisa failure? Obviously not.

Did Apple give up on the market of keyboardless mobile equipment, or after the Newton failure? Obviously, not: the iPad, with its touch screen, can be considered as a distant follow-up of the Newton, even though (probably based on Newton's return of experience), the stylus was summarily dismissed by Jobs as a suitable input device, until a new technology for a professional graphics device (the iPad Pro) could come of age in 2015. Apple subsequently rehabilited and repositioned the stylus as a precision designer's pen.

Did Apple give up on the camera market, after the QuickTake failure? Obviously not, but the camera functionality is now considered as an integral part of other products, smartphones or tablets.

Did Apple give up on the video game market, after the Pippin failure? For the time being, yes.

Did Apple give up on the TV market, after the failure of the Macintosh TV? Obviously not, the Apple TV is there.

Did Apple give up on the market of the high-end professional computer after the G Cube failure? Obviously not, the Mac Pro is now there that strangely resembles a former product.

Many other examples could have been given, these are the most significant. Indeed, Apple may encounter failure (even though the G Cube in this list is the only Apple 2.0 product, launched after Steve Jobs returned to stewardship). With the exception of the video game market so far, Apple managed in every case to make such a comeback – successful comeback that the initial failure has been totally wiped out and resigned oblivion.

However, in each of the cases, the comeback took many years to happen, all the lessons from the previous failure had been learned. And the new offering is totally different from its failed predecessor.

Perseverance is not stubbornness.

As said, the only exception in this failure list is the video game market. Could it be that Apple size is now such that this market makes it negligible for Apple? Or, perhaps, that the notion of a specialized video game device may be just a temporary remnant of the past?

In the TV case, the Apple TV is an unusually modest move, presented as a "hobby". But, it may well be that this is just the beginning, as the story is not over.

---

Gene **AAPL013 – Practice perseverance.**

*Success requires perseverance. Not to be confused with stubbornness.*

---

Very often, the main obstacle to improvement is the incapacity of the leaders to recognize that they made a mistake. Leaders do not reach the top level of a large company without a strong feeling of their superiority. This not only has some positive aspects, in the sense that the person is immune to any doubts, but also negative aspects, because such a psychological profile is not typically prone to self-criticism.

Experience shows that companies internally developing a strong feeling of superiority are in great danger, because that feeling is both a cause and an early sign of possible coming decline. Everybody has examples in mind.

Furthermore, it is very hard for a leader to recognize a failure for which he bears no responsibility.

Few high level leaders remain humble enough to apologize in public, and accept personal responsibility for failures. Tim Cook did so at the occasion of the troublesome Plans application launch. This tells us a lot about Apple's DNA.

> ### Gene **AAPL014 – Failure today breeds tomorrow's success.**
>
> *Recognizing a failure is a tough act for a leader. Arguably the only way to make progress.*

# 8

# On Research and Development

## 8.1. The chasm

Research and development (R&D) is that self-centered activity that underpins tomorrow's technological edge. Here is an, often internal, activity that, if not secret, at least arguably deserves protecting its results, if only it were to safeguard the usufruct of what it yields.

And this may explain why R&D may have been shielded from sight, having had corporate forms becoming entrenched silos. IBM conducted vast research activity that it published about, but in a form that nobody could directly exploit. In its voluminous annual "Technical Disclosure" books, IBM customarily published the past ideas and inventions and let them enter the public domain immediately, thus making them not protectable anymore. Which was also a way to neutralize lurking competition in areas outside of its direct interest.

Furthermore, there still exists that eternally conflicting marketing-research rapport within firms. A poisonous divide that renders them somewhat schizophrenic sometimes.

### 8.1.1. *Business school*

The marketing department specifies the products to be developed, while the technical teams develop them accordingly.

R&D sources innovation.

Whatever the complexity of technology, marketing is the way to push it to people not intelligent enough to use it.

Find a market for that product (push); fill that market with a product (pull).

### 8.1.2. *Apple*

Targeted customer experience dictates technical R&D issues to solve, associated with new product lines introduction. The objective is to come up with an insanely great product. The rest is either granted or secondary.

Technology made simple to use enables human capacities and frees evolutionary operations.

## 8.2. Amplifying the gap and progressing

You just cannot stop technology. Technology is convoluted to human evolution.

An initial remark is that R&D spending figures in general are to be taken with "a grain of salt", because it is very tempting for a CEO to disguise a loss into an R&D expenditure, or to pad R&D expenditures, because of tax credit incentive considerations.

Even though Apple R&D expenditures have significantly increased in absolute terms, (http://www.aboveavalon.com/notes/2015/5/3/significant-rd-increase-suggests-apple-is-working-on-something-big), they remain amazingly low as a turnover percentage, for a high tech company.

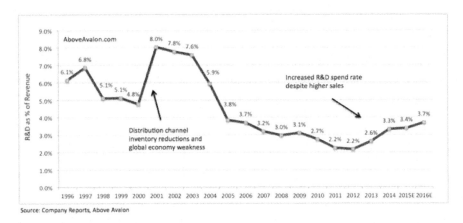

Source: Company Reports, Above Avalon

**Figure 8.1.** *Apple's R&D spending versus revenue over the years shows usual trend*

Some people explain this by the incredibly small size of Apple's product portfolio. And indeed, Apple makes almost $200B turnover with a set of products which can be all displayed on a single tabletop.

Yet, this amazing hallmark does not explain everything, because the number of product lines is less significant than the number of underlying technologies on which these products are based.

Under a small volume, a smartphone is a huge combination of various technologies, in rapid evolution. Identifying the right patents which may impact successful design choices is a major technical and legal headache.

Apple is a system integrator which outsources from other companies most of the components of its products. A situation that brings the considerable advantage of letting these external firms support the corresponding huge R&D costs.

However, on a small, and yet growing number of key technologies (for example, its Advanced RISC Machine (ARM) processors), Apple develops its own R&D, soon identified as a market differentiating factor.

The growth of Apple R&D expenditures is also related to this vertical integration, which widens the R&D perimeter.

Do not confuse this trend with the old *"make or buy"* strategy dilemma purported by traditional business schools, because Apple does not manufacture anything directly. The scope is more *"design internally"* versus *"delegate the design"*.

It is also noteworthy that, when designing a high-tech device to be mass produced, many key requirements related to its "productibility" have to be taken into account. It is amazing that Apple, which does not produce anything else other than software, owns such a deep expertise on these producibility issues.

In cases where Apple decides to develop its own technology, this frequently implies the acquisition of a start-up company.

It is a common belief that buying a company is the easiest thing in the world, especially if you have Apple's deep pockets. In fact, identifying the appropriate target, the maturity of its technology, and its long-term potential, is a daunting task, almost as difficult as developing the corresponding technology.

Compared with other companies' track records of huge acquisition prices, Apple's extraordinary talent to identify the technologies of the future, and to acquire them, at a reasonable price, and before its competitors, even having nobody notice, is stunning.

Also stunning is the speed at which the acquisitions translate into tangible benefits in Apple's product line.

In the world of start-up acquisitions, failures are quite frequent, and developing innovative products is not just as simple as writing a cheque.

Some large companies have an original approach to technology watch, in setting up a venture capital structure usually based in Silicon Valley, and in principle only dedicated to making equity investments in promising starts-up. A positive side-effect of this is that, without having to make any prospection effort, these outfits are approached by candidate start-ups looking for money. A move that returns those companies' most accurate technological and business information, and for free. We are not aware of a dedicated similar Apple structure.

On this subject, as well as on another, the figures denote Apple's extreme selectivity. Contrary to competitors dispersing their efforts across a large number of exploratory subjects without any clear outcome, Apple is focused on well-identified areas, which always directly relate to desirable product improvements.

When comparing the R&D amount spent by some large groups, on the one hand, and their innovations launched on the market on the other hand – even taking into account at the necessary time lag – we frequently get the impression that the R&D is just an alibi. The $9B per year of Microsoft R&D spending remains hard to see in its product pipeline.

In fact, Steve Jobs made a clear statement about this:

> "*Innovation has nothing to do with how many R&D dollars you have. When Apple came up with the Mac, IBM was spending at least 100 times more on R&D. It's not about money. It's about the people you have, how you're led, and how much you get it.*"

Steve Jobs in *Fortune* (9 November 1998)
Also quoted in "TIME digital 50" in *TIME* digital archive (1999)

From a process maturity standpoint, we can conclude that the technology change management (TCM) process (see Appendix 2) is mastered at a very high level at Apple, and that it is of course a key success driver for a high tech company.

Behind this impressive achievement stands necessarily in the back, for each Apple product, a long-term roadmap, which is probably the most secret part of this already secret company.

In its Global Innovation 1000 Survey, Booz Allen Hamilton consultants demonstrated for the first time since 2005, a blatant decorrelation between R&D budgets and the qualitative perception of the capacity to innovate. When considering sales growth versus indexed R&D-to-sales ratio, Apple appears as out abnormal. They even added that "*in 495 such analyses, similarly uncorrelated results for profitability growth, enterprise profitability (gross, operating, and net), market capitalization growth, and total shareholder return demonstrated that R&D spending has little or no impact on these indicators of success*".

A then puzzling discovery which led A. Hatchuel to declare: "*Innovation policy can't be reduced to merely managing R&D; it's a strategic activity possessing an own governance*".

---

Gene **AAPL015 – R&D is a means, not an end.**

*The product roadmap drives the entire R&D effort.*

Gene **AAPL016 – Decouple R&D spending from innovation spending.**

*Technology change management includes an acquisition policy which must outrun competitors.*

---

# On Company Acquisition

## 9.1. The chasm

We have seen how important acquiring external assets for large companies which are technology thirsty is. The motivation looks simple when catching up with competition or erecting entry barriers for dangerous competitors. After all, acquiring is controlling, at least on paper. But, does an acquisition strategy amounting to quick gains or long losses?

### 9.1.1. *Business school*

The CEO must seize any opportunity to buy competitors, to increase the market share. The necessary effort to reach product line convergence is estimated and engaged after the acquisition. In some cases, it may compromise the financial interest of the operation. Coming across the situation by then is too late....

### 9.1.2. *Apple*

Market share is not the fundamental objective. When buying a company which, as a start-up, frequently has no market share at all, the only thing that matters is the potential of its technology for the product lines of the company, and the time to market gained by acquiring it. The offering of the acquired company, if any, is immediately withdrawn from the market, to become an Apple exclusive differentiating factor.

Apple never buys a company based on its established market share.

### 9.2. Amplifying the gap

Table 9.1 is borrowed from Wikipedia and shows the list of companies acquired by Apple since 1988. It traces the historical acquisitions made by Apple over most of its history. What is striking is to see they most often hit the bull's eye in terms of long-term strategy, respective to the company's ecosystem of products. Always accruing value to the whole, while bringing a distinctive merit. Which merit was transformed into worth?

| Number | Date | Company | Business | Value (USD) | Derived products |
|---|---|---|---|---|---|
| 1 | March 2, 1988 | Network Innovations | Software | | – |
| 2 | June 7, 1988 | Orion Network Systems | Satellite communication systems | – | – |
| 3 | June 27, 1988 | Styleware | Computer software | – | AppleWorks GS |
| 4 | July 11, 1988 | Nashoba Systems | Computer software | – | FileMaker |
| 5 | January 3, 1989 | Coral Software | Computer software | – | – |
| 6 | February 7, 1997 | NeXT | Computer programming services | US$404,000,000 | OS X, iOS |

| | | | | | |
|---|---|---|---|---|---|
| 7 | September 2, 1997 | Power Computing Corporation | Clone computers | US$110,000,000 | – |
| 8 | January 8, 1999 | Xemplar Education | Software | US$4,926,000 | – |
| 9 | November 3, 1999 | Raycer Graphics | Computer graphic chips | US$15,000,000 | – |
| 10 | January 7, 2000 | NetSelector | Internet software | – | – |
| 11 | April 11, 2000 | Astarte-DVD Authoring Software | Software | – | DVD Studio Pro |
| 12 | 2000 (Q4) | SoundJam MP | Software | – | iTunes |
| 13 | 2001 | Bluefish Labs | Productivity software | – | iWork |
| 14 | May 11, 2001 | Bluebuzz | Internet service provider (ISP) | – | – |
| 15 | July 9, 2001 | Spruce Technologies | Graphics software | US$14,900,000 | DVD Studio Pro |
| 16 | December 31, 2001 | PowerSchool | Online info systems services | US$66,100,000 | PowerSchool |
| 17 | February 1, 2002 | Nothing Real | Special effects software | US$15,000,000 | Shake |
| 18 | April 4, 2002 | Zayante | FireWire chips and software | US$13,000,000 | FireWire |

| | | | | | |
|---|---|---|---|---|---|
| 19 | June 11, 2002 | Silicon Grail Corp-Chalice [note 7] | Digital effects software | US$20,000,000 | Final Cut Pro |
| 20 | June 20, 2002 | Propel Software | Software | – | – |
| 21 | June 21, 2002 | Prismo Graphics | Special-effects titling software for film and video | US$20,000,000 | LiveType (Final Cut Studio) |
| 22 | July 1, 2002 | Emagic | Music production software | US$30,000,000 | Logic Pro, GarageBand |
| 23 | March 2005 | Schemasoft | Software | – | iWork |
| 24 | April 2005 | FingerWorks | Gesture recognition company | – | iOS |
| 25 | October 16, 2006 | Silicon Color | Software | – | Color (Final Cut Studio) |
| 26 | December 4, 2006 | Proximity | Software | – | Final Cut Server |
| 27 | April 24, 2008 | P.A. Semi | Semiconductors | US$278,000,000 | Apple SOC |
| 28 | July 7, 2009 | Placebase | Maps | – | Maps |
| 29 | December 6, 2009 | Lala.com | Music streaming | US$17,000,000 | iCloud, iTunes Match |
| 30 | January 5, 2010 | Quattro Wireless | Mobile advertising | US$275,000,000 | iAd |
| 31 | April 27, | Intrinsity | Semiconductors | US$121,000,000 | Apple SOC |

| | | | | | |
|---|---|---|---|---|---|
| | 2010 | | | | |
| 32 | April 27, 2010 | Siri | Voice control software | – | Siri |
| 33 | July 14, 2010 | Poly9 | Web-based mapping | – | Maps |
| 34 | September 20, 2010 | Polar Rose | Facial recognition | US$29,000,000 | iOS |
| 35 | September 14, 2010 | IMSense | High-dynamic-range (HDR) photography | – | iOS |
| 36 | August 1, 2011 | C3 Technologies | 3D mapping | US$267,000,000 | Maps |
| 37 | December 20, 2011 | Anobit | Flash memory | US$390,000,000 | iPod, iPhone, iPad |
| 38 | February 23, 2012 | Chomp | App search engine | US$50,000,000 | App Store |
| 39 | June 2, 2012 | Redmatica | Audio | – | Logic Pro |
| 40 | July 27, 2012 | AuthenTec | PC and mobile security products | US$356,000,000 | Touch ID |
| 41 | September 27, 2012 | Particle | HTML5 Web app firm | – | iCloud, iAd |
| 42 | 2013 | Novauris Technologies | Speech recognition | – | Siri |
| 43 | 2013 | OttoCat | Search engine | – | App Store |
| 44 | March 23, 2013 | WiFiSlam | Indoor location | US$20,000,000 | Maps |

| 45 | July 19, 2013 | Locationary | Maps | – | Maps |
|---|---|---|---|---|---|
| 46 | July 19, 2013 | HopStop.com | Maps | – | Maps |
| 47 | August 1, 2013 | Passif Semiconductor | Semiconductors | – | – |
| 48 | August 13, 2013 | Matcha | Media discovery app | – | – |
| 49 | August 22, 2013 | Embark | Maps | – | Maps |
| 50 | August 28, 2013 | AlgoTrim | Data compression | – | – |
| 51 | October 3, 2013 | Cue | Personal assistant | US$50,000,000 | – |
| 52 | November 24, 2013 | PrimeSense | Semiconductors | US$345,000,000 | – |
| 53 | December 2, 2013 | Topsy | Analytics | US$200,000,000 | – |
| 54 | December 23, 2013 | BroadMap | Maps | – | Maps |
| 55 | December 23, 2013 | Catch.com | Software | – | – |
| 56 | January 4, 2014 | SnappyLabs | Photography software | – | Camera |
| 57 | February 21, 2014 | Burstly | Software | – | App Testing and Distribution |
| 58 | May 2, 2014 | LuxVue Technology | micro-LED displays | – | – |

| 59 | June 6, 2014 | Spotsetter | Social search engine | – | Maps |
|---|---|---|---|---|---|
| 60 | June 29, 2014 | Swell | Music streaming | US$30,000,000 | iTunes |
| 61 | June 29, 2014 | BookLamp | Software | – | iBooks |
| 62 | August 1, 2014 | Beats Electronics | Headphones, music streaming (Beats Music) | US$3,000,000,000 | iPhone, iTunes |
| 63 | September 23, 2014 | Prss | Digital magazine | – | – |
| 64 | 2014 | Dryft | Keyboard App | – | – |
| 65 | January 21, 2015 | Semetric | Music analytics | US$50,000,000 | iTunes Radio, Beats Music |
| 66 | March 24, 2015 | Foundation DB | Database | – | iCloud |
| 67 | April 14, 2015 | LinX | Camera | US$20,000,000 | iPod, iPhone, iPad |

**Table 9.1.** *Apple's acquisitions through history: a cornucopia of long-term value, most of the time brought in right on target and soon transformed into worthwhile internal assets (source: https://en.wikipedia. org/wiki/List_of_ mergers_and_acquisitions_by_Apple)*

In most cases, a company acquisition remains unknown to the public, and surfaces only in the financial reporting associated with quarterly result presentation meetings.

In those rare cases where the acquisition gets known to the public, Apple either denies or confirms, in the latter case with the ritual pithy statement:

> *"Apple buys smaller technology companies from time to time and we generally do not discuss our purpose or plans."*

## 9.3. Progressing the gap

Upon reading Table 9.1, the following general comments can be made:

*– Acquisition rate.*

The first observation is that Apple's company acquisition rate has significantly increased over the last years, up to about one company every two months, according to a 2013 statement by Tim Cook.

This may well be due to the ever-more complex nature of each single product, thus requiring an increased ability to spot sophisticated components, which may focus ever-more on tinier ever domains of R&D. Company buyers see their role evolve: they find themselves at the heart of ecosystems of becoming, anticipating trends, facilitating innovation processes, and promoting markets. Far beyond adjusting an existing offer and demand, they open up new avenues for offer and demand to operate in.

In the case of Maps, a clear sourcing effort was performed to get a proper solution to the customer discontent that was initially voiced.

*– Price paid.*

It can be seen that by Californian high-tech industry standards, acquisition prices remain modest. NeXT acquisition, which resulted in Steve Jobs coming back, was negotiated by Apple for $400M, an almost ridiculous amount compared with the $3.2B paid by Google for the Nest acquisition. The only acquisition above 1 B$ is the one of Beats.

This shows that Apple manages to acquire companies by the time their technology just gets promising: when it is clearly proven, feasibility being out of question, and at the same time when it has not entered market. A scrupulous sense of timing that translates into a magic wand.

*– Success.*

There is arguably no operation in this list which has been reported as a total failure. And, given the appetite of the press for Apple failures, this can be considered as a good criterion for rating success pending acquisition.

It may also happen that Apple disengages from some companies it has invested in, but this case is very unusual. There are only two occurrences for the totality of the period. One was Misys Plc's MCM (Misys Computer Maintenance division), which acquired the maintenance activities of Basingstoke-based Apple Computer Inc systems specialist Sign Express Group Ltd in 1992. The other is SCI Systems, which purchased Apple's manufacturing facility located at 702 Bandley Drive, Fountain, Colorado ("Fountain") in 1996, with certain related assets.

There was also a partial divestiture through which Apple shares in ARM – a company formerly known as Advanced RISC Machines – fell to 14.8% in 1999.

In summary, technologies acquired rapidly find their way into Apple products.

Such a rate of success is remarkable, and we would say, stunning.

---

Gene **AAPL017 – Acquire the right company at the right time.**

*Technology change management includes an acquisition policy which must outrun the competitors.*

---

# The Manager, the Software and the Process

## 10.1. The chasm

There are hardware companies and there are software companies. And there are software people and hardware people. The curse of the computing industry since the early days is such: companies have to choose their camp, between those who perceive themselves as primarily hardware organizations, and those who perceive themselves as primarily software organizations.

Why is it that only Apple has taken both sides since its inception? And sustained the unification of both sides throughout its history? Because both Steve Jobs and Wozniak had a passion for designing computing machines? Or just by thinking *differently?*

### 10.1.1. *Business school way*

The manager treats software like any other technical activity, through the commitments taken by software people. However, after several years of experience, he usually comes to the conclusion that software is a never ending source of trouble, and for some strange reason, always lives on a critical path.

Software people are regarded as disreputable, unreliable, always carrying a source of problems and unable to provide visibility about their work.

Furthermore, as is often the case, the company does not have the internal expertise and resources to develop the required software.

The traditional manager will therefore find many good reasons to get rid of the software hassle, by outsourcing it, and much more systematically than he does for other hardware components.

In spite of its associated cost (undoubtedly real), the immaterial nature of the software anchors, in an incompetent manager's head, the idea that software "cannot be serious", just a necessary evil.

An MBA degree is the golden key for accessing to top-level management, and managers are frequently poured in from outside. Under no circumstances can a software manager reach the top level.

### 10.1.2. *Apple's way*

Software is just like any other engineering discipline, and it is considered critical enough to be produced internally. The fact is that it is the only thing which Apple produces internally.

Software managers may reach the top level, if they demonstrate they deserve it. There is no predefined path to reach the top level, apart from a demonstrated track record of success.

All managers, including the top-level ones, understand software specificities, do not fall into the usual traps and do not despise software and those who develop it.

### 10.2. Developing the chasm

For a manager with an MBA degree, without any other technical experience, managing software teams is no different from managing any other team: what only matters is to negotiate the team commitments, and to keep track of these, with appropriate periodicity.

Of course, during the commitment negotiation, it is the manager's role and duty to exert adequate pressure on the teams, and rejects any funding request which would not directly contribute to the production of code, which, as everybody can understand, is the only thing which matters.

In spite of what seems to be the common sense nature of the following, this attitude can lead to nothing but major project failures – and experience shows that *IT DOES LEAD* – for a number of reasons we would like to detail now. These are but ultimately rooted, unless exception, in global manager ignorance about the very nature of software activities.

This widespread ignorance can be explained by four basic considerations:

1) Software has frequently crept into the products, in such a gradual mode that managers did not take notice.

2) The software product is immaterial.

3) Software development is made up of activities of a totally unknown nature to the manager.

4) Even more than for other activities, huge productivity discrepancies may exist among programmers.

Appendix 2 discusses each of the above points so as to provide the necessary background for understanding the true power status of software better.

### 10.2.1. *The case of Mister Hullot*

Jean-Marie Hullot graduated from Ecole Normale Supérieure (ENS Rue d'Ulm in Paris), a small institution by size, but a genuine "Fields Medal nursery[1]".

Thanks to Jean-Marie Hullot, Apple could prepare the grounds for entering a future booming mobile telephone business, long before that took place. Hullot was Chief Technology Officer (CTO) of the Apple Applications Division from 2001 to 2005, and in this position, managed the iCalc and iSync Apple development teams for Mac OS X in 2002.

Steve Jobs called up Jean-Marie Hullot directly in Paris. Jean-Marie is famous in the NeXT developer community for being one of the creators of the NeXTStep Interface Builder (IB) tool. IB is considered by some as a "killer app" on NeXTStep, which allowed the user to rapidly manipulate and assemble software objects (either

---

1 The Fields Medal is the equivalent of the Nobel prize for mathematicians.

its own ones or those built by others) into useful programs without writing any code. IB lives on today in the free developer tool set that Apple provides.

At that time, the offices occupied by Jean-Marie Hullot team were located on the Avenue des Champs Elysées, in Paris, a considerably more luxurious location than the one of the French Apple Headquarters.

The call to Hullot was initially an audio conversation. He was then living near the Eiffel Tower and, at Steve Job's request, attached a firewire video camera. When Steve disconnected the audio call, iChatAV on Steve's computer recognized that a video camera was available. When Steve Jobs called back, the call became both video and audio.

But, French people do not leave their country so easily, and this collaboration came to an end when Steve Jobs, given the strategic importance of these developments, decided to bring them back to California.

Jean-Marie Hullot's Wikipedia page (in English) only mentions his PhD, but not his quality of Ecole Normale Supérieure Rue d'Ulm graduate, which is immensely more significant in French credential hierarchy (see, for example, [HUL 15]). Jean-Marie was also President and CEO of Fotopedia, a famous and visionary collaborative photo encyclopedia, which he created.

So, instead of concluding that the bad programmers must be fired, it is wiser to hire the best, and if possible, like Steve Jobs did, the geniuses.

### 10.2.2. Drawing lessons from software management

Is there not a contradiction between the above story, which insists on hiring the best software personnel on the one hand, and the "process approach" of software described in Appendix 2 (see later) on the other hand, which considers coding activity as something of minor importance, which can be handled by people swapping one for another at will?

At first sight, yes. But, this apparent contradiction is based on a misunderstanding of what is meant by "coding". Software development is probably the only activity (with craftsmanship) where product design cannot be separated from product realization. The "good" software developer can be good at coding – and this is often the case – but he/she is first a "good" architect and a "good" designer, because his/her talent in this latter design tasks makes the difference.

This leads us to a final comment on this subject. As far as we can tell, Michelangelo was not very demanding in his work, to say the least, as he was totally absorbed by his artistic achievements.

If a company aims at attracting the best software people, and at sustaining their motivation all along the demanding development phases – something that may imply huge personal life sacrifices – a corresponding reward is necessary.

Each and every social system may find different ways to satisfy this, and some may be better than others, according to this criterion.

What is true, for sure, is that considering the programmer as a kind of modern day scribe or perhaps slave, paid (as little as possible) by the number of lines of code produced, can only result in poor software quality, of any possible standard, and far from the excellence target Steve Jobs had in mind.

A "software illiterate" manager's contempt for software, and for those who develop it, is a royal path to failure.

It has been reported that at NeXT, Steve Jobs used to hire PhDs as receptionists. Without going to such an extreme, it should be possible to find an acceptable level of expertise and salary for the people to be hired as programmers.

---

Gene **AAPL018 – Software is a powerful force.**

*Software pushes other technology types around; therefore balances power within enterprises.*

Gene **AAPL019 – Software differentiates.**

*Regard software as a differentiating factor, not as a commodity.*

Gene **AAPL020 – Software is different development.**

*Software development presents a fundamental management issue.*
*A modern manager must understand software specificities.*

Gene **AAPL021 – Respect software status and software people.**

*Good software cannot be built on top of contempt for software developers.*

Gene **AAPL022 – Process software.**

*Mastering the software development process is not in contradiction with hiring exceptional, off-the-scale talent.*

---

*"The more I see, the less I know for sure."*
John Lennon

# Emergence of a Brand: From Failures to Everyday Situations (*In Search of Exclusive Value*)

# Failures Left Behind

## 11.1. Why failures?

By common standards, a failure is a negative experience that should be avoided by all means. It leaves bad impressions, psychological traces and is hard to recover from. But, how do we learn, if not from failures? A child's ability to learn is fully based on failures; why not take stock of our biological nature to improve all that we do and forever?

*But, wait a minute,* says our consciousness (which is hard). *We deserve some rest after our successes, which we acquired at a high cost.*

### 11.1.1. *Business school*

– A failure is a negative experience that should be avoided by all means.

– Standard pitch: avoid failure, pursue wealth and resolve the short-term first.

### 11.1.2. *Apple*

Failed often. Badly. Unquestionably.

Own way: fail many times. Pursue insightful things with intensity.

## 11.2. Failure dissolves in time

There is intrinsic heaviness in being successful. You may avoid failure for a long time, but you will become heavy. This drives innovation out of industry.

The lightness of being a beginner again makes you less sure about everything but makes you free to pursue creativity. Get something and understand it thoroughly. This brings innovation in.

With intensity, time loses its linearity. Time is not linear. What counts is what happens tomorrow. Think long-term.

## 11.3. A basket of historical failures

Below is a quick recap of a collection of memorable fiascos and aborted projects that went, for the most part, into oblivion. Going past revisiting them is instructing, more: an obligation, should we endeavor to trace the attitude *a posteriori* taken with respect to the corresponding products. The following historical excerpts are from Wikipedia.

*1983: The Apple Lisa*

**Figure 11.1.** *LISA, the metaphoric "self-driving computer", equipped with point and click features as a 1983 advertisement suggested (source: http://archive.wired. com/gadgets/mac/ multimedia/2008/01/gallery_apple_flops?slide=4&slideView=2)*

The Lisa was an attempt to follow the success Apple had with the Apple II. It failed, and the Lisa remains one of the most notorious examples of Apple hubris. Granted, it was the first personal computer to have a Graphical User Interface (GUI) and a mouse, but Apple strayed significantly from its overriding ethos of making affordable personal computers when it released this business-oriented computer. When it debuted in 1983, Lisa (which was either named after Steve Jobs' first daughter or stood for "Local Integrated Software Architecture") cost a whopping $9,995 – or $20,807.06 in today's dollars. Needless to say, the Lisa did not sell very well. Businesses opted for less-expensive IBM PCs, which were already dominating business desktop computing. The Lisa was finally canned in August 1986, by which time Apple's more affordable Macintosh had already become a bona-fide hit.

> Gene **AAPL023 – Reveal markets indirectly.**
>
> *Use that one terrible failure as bait revealing the "truer market".*

*1993: The Messagepad (or The Newton)*

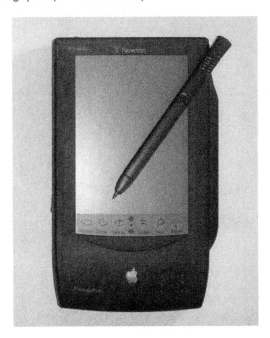

**Figure 11.2.** *The so-called Newton pad had a stylus and could access databases (source: http://archive.wired.com/gadgets/mac/multimedia/ 2008/01/gallery_apple_flops?slide=4&slideView=2)*

Arguably, the most famous Apple flop of all, the Newton (which was actually the name of the OS and not the device) started out as a top-secret project with a lofty goal: to reinvent personal computing. During its development, the Newton took on many forms, such as the tablet-like "Cadillac" prototype, before its eventual release in 1993 as a smaller and considerably less revolutionary PDA (Personal Digital Assistant). Although the Newton was available for 6 years (longer than most other Apple flops), it was a prime example of an idea that was simply ahead of its time, and sales never lived up to Apple's expectations. When Steve Jobs resumed his stewardship of Apple in 1997, one of the first things he did was to axe the subsidiary Newton Systems Group. By the following February, the Newton was dead.

---

Gene **AAPL024 – Good idea requires right timing.**

*Bad timing doesn't imply bad idea. A good idea must wait the time comes for it.*

---

*1993: The Macintosh TV*

**Figure 11.3.** *The Macintosh TV was made by assembling a Sony Trinitron TV and an Apple Performa computer (source: http://archive.wired.com/ gadgets/mac/multimedia/2008/01/gallery_apple_flops?slide=4&slideView=2)*

Long before the Apple TV and iTunes were a glimmer in Steve Jobs' eye, there was Macintosh TV. Clad in all black, the Macintosh TV was the unholy fusion of a 14-inch, cable-ready Sony Trinitron television and an Apple Performa 520. Introduced in 1993, the Macintosh TV was discontinued the following year. Its major failing: it was incapable of showing television feeds in a desktop window. In the end, only 10,000 units were ever produced. Apple continued to experiment with small form factor PCs with the subsequent G4 Cube and eventually saw some success with its all-in-one iMac design in 1998.

---

Gene **AAPL025 – Blend form and function.**

*As medium is message, a form factor carries meaning. But it should be aligned with content, i.e. function.*

---

*1994: The Apple Quicktake*

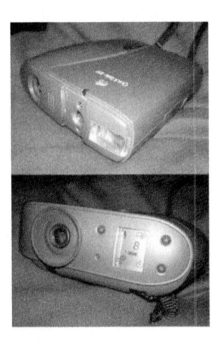

**Figure 11.4.** *The Venus codenamed QuickTake camera connected to any Macintosh computer (source: http://archive.wired.com/gadgets/mac/multimedia/2008/01/gallery_apple_flops?slide=4&slideView=2)*

In 1992, Apple Computer started marketing plans for a digital camera called QuickTake, codenamed Venus. The QuickTake 100 was released in 1994 as an easy-to-use digital camera that connected to any Macintosh computer by way of an Apple serial cable. The camera was capable of storing eight photos at 640 × 480 resolution, 32 photos at 320 × 240 resolution or a mixture of both sizes. All photos were at 24-bit color.

It was one of the first digital cameras released targeted to consumers.

The QuickTake 150 kit included a separate close-up lens that allowed focusing at approximately 30 cm. Apple offered a factory upgrade to the QuickTake 100 changing the name to the QuickTake 100 Plus, which included all the functionality of the QuickTake 150.

Apple released a connection kit for Microsoft Windows with the QuickTake 150 in 1995. The last QuickTake model was the Fujifilm-built QuickTake 200, released in 1996. The 200 added focus and aperture controls, as well as the ability to store images on removable SmartMedia flashRAM cards.

The various QuickTake models did not sell very well, as other companies such as Kodak, Fujifilm, Canon and Nikon entered the digital market with brands that consumers associated with photography. They were discontinued in 1997 shortly after Steve Jobs returned to Apple. In an attempt to streamline Apple's operations, Jobs discontinued many non-computer products, including the Newton line of products, the LaserWriter printer line and the QuickTake cameras.

The Apple QuickTake camera has since become a collector's item for Apple enthusiasts.

---

A repeat. See:

Gene **AAPL024. – Good idea requires right timing.**

---

*1996: The Apple Pippin*

**Figure 11.5.** *The video game player PIPPIN had a very advanced form factor yet failed miserably (source: http://archive.wired.com/gadgets/mac/ multimedia/2008/01 /gallery_apple_flops?slide=4&slideView=2)*

Very few people seem to remember that Apple made an attempt to penetrate the video game market with the Pippin in 1996 – and failed miserably. As a multimedia platform marketed by Apple and toy-maker Bandai, the Pippin was an attempt to create an inexpensive machine that could play games and serve as a network computer. The device tanked for myriad reasons: lack of software, misbranding and the fact that the market was already dominated by systems such as the Nintendo 64, Sega and the Sony PlayStation.

A repeat. See:

Gene **AAPL025 – Blend form and function.**

*2000: The G4 Cube*

**Figure 11.6.** *The Jonathan Ive-designed 8 x 8 x 8-inch Cube addressed designers and web professionals (source: http://archive.wired.com/gadgets/ mac/multimedia/2008/01/gallery_apple_flops?slide=5&slideView=2)*

Still a highly sought-after collectors' item, the Jonathan Ive-designed Cube never quite caught on with the people it was supposed to entice: designers and web professionals. The 8×8×8-inches Cube was supposed to fill the gap between the iMac G3 and the Power Mac G4 but was lambasted by critics for its lack of a monitor and high price tag. This led to slow sales, which never really picked up.

Eventually, the Cube faded into obscurity – but only after Ive won several international awards for its design.

The result: everything has a meaning, be it outside or inside. Meaning is in everything. No wonder the first Macintosh series had the signatures of each member of the team engraved within the cover.

---

Gene **AAPL026 – Meaning is everything.**

*A form factor that isn't balanced with function relegates to decoration.*

---

Table 11.1 recaps the four genes found in scanning a number of Apple's major historical failures.

---

Gene **AAPL023 – Reveal markets indirectly.**

*Use that terrible failure as bait revealing the "truer market".*

Gene **AAPL024 – Good idea requires right timing.**

*Bad timing doesn't imply bad idea. A good idea must wait the time comes for it.*

Gene **AAPL025 – Blend form and function.**

*As medium is message, a form factor carries meaning. But it should be aligned with content, i.e. function.*

Gene **AAPL026 – Meaning is everything.**

*A form factor that isn't balanced with function relegates to decoration.*

---

**Table 11.1.** *A list of four genes corresponding to Apple's major historical failures*

# A Cornucopia of Commerce Situations

There are actually many situations which lead to antagonizing traditional thinking and Apple thinking. In this chapter, we provide a list of thematic situations which pave the way toward more in-depth investigation.

## 12.1. Commercial policy

### 12.1.1. *Business school*

– Provide salesman a bonus incentive based on turnover.

– Concentrate on increasing market share, by all means.

### 12.1.2. *Apple*

– Concentrate on customer satisfaction, and disregard the rest.

## 12.2. Asking customers

### 12.2.1. *Business school*

– Stick to your customers. Be as close as possible, so you know your customer better than the customer knows himself, or herself.

– Start from the technology and create customer experience.

### 12.2.2. *Apple*

– Do not ask your customers. They do not know the future, nor what they will want.

– Detach yourself from the present conditions.

### 12.2.3. *Development*

Your customers are tied in present conditions and cannot extract themselves from them. You will be tied same wise as soon as you abide with these.

Start with customer experience and work back toward the technology.

**Figure 12.1.** *Typography at Apple: when medium is message (souce: http://www.applegazette.com/mac/the-typography-of-apple-typeface-design-from-1984-to-today-info-graphic/)*

## 12.3. Forecasting and strategy

### 12.3.1. *Business school*

– Forecast and then specify your market line.

### 12.3.2. *Apple*

– Feel the direction and maintain it as long as the feeling remains.

### 12.3.3. *Development*

Feel your inner voice.

Mainframes in the 1970s, PCs in the 1980s, mobile computing in the 2000s and Internet of Things in the mid-2010s: a planner's skyrocketing curve never forecasts a future reality.

Forecasting returns the echo from others' doing. Does it sound right for you? Forecasting does not explain why it looks so. So, you follow a consequence while not knowing the cause. Example, connecting objects is a big trend. But, what is your vision in connecting them? Which objects? Why and for doing what?

## 12.4. Grabbing a trend

### 12.4.1. *Business school*

– If market improves, grab a slice and …*"catch me if you can!"*

### 12.4.2. *Apple*

– Detach from mainstream.

### 12.4.3. *Development*

– The PC story with PC compatibles and software powered by Microsoft.

– Own your trend.

When markets grow, their DNA is owned by somebody else and you are bound to their genes. You grow a comfort zone that is complacency on somebody else comfort.

## 12.5. Communicating

### 12.5.1. *Business school*

Communicate with mantras.

### 12.5.2. *Apple*

Put the mantra inside the product.

### 12.5.3. *Development*

"*Mantra inside*" everything? Even down to the character font (see Figure 12.1).

Communication is a reflection from the product, and not of the product. Thus, you have to manage the alignment of the two. Satisfy the customer, and then let them manage the communication about your products: they will exhibit the mantra inside.

## 12.6. Getting incomparable value

### 12.6.1. *Business school*

Benchmark yourself against your competitors.

Confront with present-day realities. Mimick. Benchmark.

### 12.6.2. *Apple*

Do not compare yourself: competitors will drift you aside, away from your core strategy. As your product is ready for launch, customers will already want something else: big loss.

Be (faithful to) yourself.

### 12.6.3. *Development*

What is your incomparability index? Product differentiation is at stakes. Sustainable differentiation is what will count.

Anticipate (Wayne Gretzky: "I skate to where the puck is going to be, not where it has been").

## 12.7. Making something profitable

### 12.7.1. *Business school*

You are well off to make something that returns profit.

Be driven by profits, if not finance.

The fiscal quarter counts first.

### 12.7.2. *Apple*

Innovate. Be driven by an idealistic perspective. In quality, time, cost (internal).

What counts is what happens tomorrow (see time).

### 12.7.3. *Development*

Me-too companies.

Create a gap.

You can change the rules when you really innovate. Therefore, you exit the ducks' pond. In the pond, profits are limited to the pond and other ducks' attitude: friends or foes. Both limit your expansion.

## 12.8. Going after the enterprise market

### 12.8.1. *Business school*

Industry structures along categories which are structured by maturing enterprises where you can find your market position.

### 12.8.2. *Apple*

Do not go for it.

### 12.8.3. *Development*

Enterprise Resource Planning (ERP) in the 1990s: the nightmare of Small and Medium Size enterprises.

Why a category designed by others should suit you? Design your own category and be free of other's structures.

Marketing was invented around the early 1980s. At that time, innovation was not developed as a focus activity as it became later since the dot com period in the late 1990s. Innovation art much matured since.

Categories are a market consensus. You do not control them, they are full with suppliers and users' habits, even bad ones. "Bad" meaning you can only compromise.

## 12.9. Expenses versus returns

### 12.9.1. *Business school*

If in trouble, cut costs, downsize, reduce X and Y.

### 12.9.2. *Apple*

Get out of the way. Do something else.

### 12.9.3. *Development*

Survival strategy is vigilance on deterioration.

The trouble is the consequence, what is the cause? A bigger issue: wrong market, wrong product or both? So, do not cure, it is a compensation for another issue. You will end up fighting and gradually deteriorating your value, even become unsellable.

## 12.10. Management to commitment to product

### 12.10.1. *Business school*

Product issues are too low-level to be in the scope of top-level managers, who have better things to do: talk to the press, investors, financial institutions, etc.

Managers are more preoccupied by their own image than by their company brand.

### 12.10.2. *Apple*

The top-level management comes up on stage to present the new products, and demonstrates through this its total commitment to success.

### 12.10.3. *Development*

Every year, at the occasion of its famous keynotes, Apple's top-level management comes up on stage to present and demonstrate the new products, like Steve Jobs used to do (although of course they cannot be as good showmen as Steve was).

Common practice? Not really. As soon as a company gets bigger, CEOs delegate such tasks, which they do not consider pertinent enough for them. Product presentation is frequently not even performed by the Head of Development, but delegated to very inferior levels of the hierarchy.

This is a disastrous signal sent to the customers. Why should they trust a manager who does not demonstrate any commitment in the products of his company?

Of course, this commitment may imply very unpleasant situations: the best example is when Steve Jobs came back from one of the few holidays he ever had with his family to handle the "Antennagate" episode.

---

Gene **AAPL027 – Top management must take charge in consumer markets.**

*In consumer goods market – whatever the size – top level management is at the front line when it comes to products.*

---

# Emergence of a Brand

## 13.1. The chasm

Branding is a classic topic in marketing education. It stands for itself as a discipline and a brand appears to be anchored on three pillars [GIG 15]:

– its vocation, which expresses its mission, representativeness and finality, i.e. *what the brand lives for*;

– its authority, which signifies its status, dignity and character, i.e. *what the brand radiates*;

– its creativity. Here lies its genius, the innovation it brings to the virtual space of words and symbols, i.e. *what does the brand leave as an imprint*.

However, when it comes to innovating, and re-innovating, the cross-pursuit game that makes competitor friction so complex is not as trivial as it may be in more stable markets. It confers branding the enhancing of its role: to be a proxy of the real thing.

Has branding become a synthetic art of doing business in a virtual space? This leads us to place branding as a last chapter drawing on previous ones. Let us take an example.

### 13.1.1. *Business school*

The leader is valued on share price. This metric is known to be volatile and subject to stock exchange dynamics, which may have little to do with actual company performance, as, by the way, any shareholder is aware of.

### 13.1.2. *Apple*

The leader is assessed on the impetus and value he manages to provide for the brand in the long-term. Of course, Steve Jobs had an eye on the AAPL stock market share price, and issued internal memos when symbolic values were reached, but nothing more.

**Figure 13.1.** *Steve Jobs: Apple Brand Purpose 1997 (source: https://www.youtube.com/watch?v=ugqcXqTEVMA)*

Figure 13.1 is extracted from a 1997 video (which included the famous "*Think Different*" ad). It is of poor image quality, yet is probably the best testimony we can find about Steve Jobs' Apple brand vision.

In the video, Steve has just returned to Apple. He has a myriad of vital things to do, and decisions to take, to keep Apple alive, which seemed an impossible task at that time.

Despite these difficulties, he takes part of his precious time to talk about the Apple brand. Steve's vision of the brand is the one of company identity, company core values. This is the way the company wants to be perceived by the public. Far from an empty mission statement which nobody cares about, it's meant to be a meaningful and stable reference point, to which any employee must feel committed.

In the above video, Steve explains that Apple *"believes people with passion can change the world"*. And that is its core value.

## 13.2. Amplifying the gap and progressing

In Appendix 5, the qualitative and quantitative concepts that establish a brand are characterized in-depth using the Trialectics methodology (an original and transdisciplinary engineering method, of thought processes that helps us to think out-of-the-box). They found the complexity of a brand, around the resulting notions of *vocation, creativity* and *authority*. The synthetic results obtained exacerbate the end point: that a brand is above all a frequency, a tune in the perceivable spectrum of all frequencies.

The complexity of a brand is best evidenced when using the Trialectics methodology. In the case of the Apple brand, Jobs cared most about a particular "frequency" that could be perceived unequivocally. More specifically:

– Apple's brand *vocation* has a representative mission, a scope breathing sustainably. Such commissioning profession has been openly demonstrated in countless public presentations.

– Its *creativity* spells innovation, genius and singularity. Little doubt that most of the firm's products bring just that.

– Finally, its *authority* is clearly backed by statute and character. The power behind the brand (e.g. through the historical logos) confers a control on the personality of the firm.

Due to Trialectics, we can now witness the extent of the match of Apple brand with an ontological notion of a brand. There has been a striking effort to forge a brand that speaks of ...a brand.

Few companies dare to address the brand issue at such an ambitious level. The brand is often left to the communications department, as a secondary logo, or unified visual identity issue, as appearing through documentation, invoices, Website, etc. Of course, these things matter too, but ultimately they may change. However, the core values do not.

Many CEOs fail to understand that, unless their personal life is worth writing books about, the general public does not care about them as individuals. They tend to mix up the promotion of their own image with the one of their company, with the ridiculous belief that once convinced of how amazing they are, the public will buy their products (even though they admit they can be lousy), and be faithful to the brand.

Would these CEOs make a public presentation in casual attire, like Steve in this video?

Although this was not the public perception when he was alive, Steve Jobs was not like these CEOs who would spend more time with the press than running their company. Steve's interviews were rather exceptional, and, most of the time, part of a product launch campaign, therefore centered around Apple and its products, and not his personal life.

With a 67% rise in Brand Value to $247 billion, Apple returned in 2015 to number one in the BrandZ™ Top 100 Most Valuable Global Brands ranking.

The value of the brand lies in the fact that the customer accepts to pay a higher price for the brand they trust, and be faithful to it.

This second aspect is something very unusual, in times where customers are known to easily switch from one supplier to another, looking for best bargain, down to every cent spared.

The strength of the Apple brand is supported by customer satisfaction rates that no Apple competitor has ever achieved: 91% for the iPad (2010), 92% for the iPhone (2007) and 97% for the Apple watch (2015) (figures published after product launch). These figures are unprecedented in mass produced consumer goods.

*"Things that were made in the past are the past."*
John Lennon

# PART 3

# Importing Apple's Genes into Transferable Knowledge
## *(In Evidence of Deeper Gaps)*

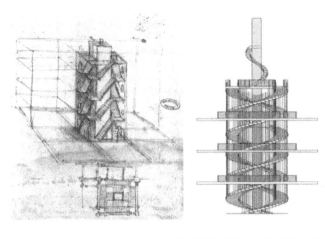

A spectacular double helix is found right at the heart of the Chambord castle in the French Loire Valley: masterpiece stairs that were, very likely according to historians, designed by Leonardo Da Vinci. A unique draft has been recovered (top left, previous page), which shows what it is like to think multidimensionnally: a quadruple spiral staircase design, while Chambord actually features only two revolutions! Two more revolutions would have meant an immense height for the ceiling, which is already huge. Other images depict variations.

Previous page – top left: 1; top right: 2; bottom left: 3; bottom right: 4.

References:

1) Top left: Leonardo Da Vinci Ms B, f. 47 r.

2) Top right: a "house car" project, described in "prix étincelle 2013" (creativity contest in partnership with *Lycées Clémenceau et Jules Verne (Nantes)*) http://prixetincelle2013.wifeo.com/axes-directeurs.php.

3) Bottom left: http://blogs.furman.edu/frn325/files/2014/11/h2-150x150.png.

4) Bottom right: Leonardo da Vinci, Drawing of a staircase Paris, Institut de France Ms B, folio 68v.

An animated contruction modeling can be found at: https://www.youtube.com/watch?v=9aYgn2fhQIU (in French).

# On Structure and Contents

Steve Jobs often appeared as a highly irrational person. Capable of an all-encompassing inspired grand vision and at the same time focused like mad on tiny implementation details that nobody before him saw. What is it that may lie behind such an impossible mixture of traits?

## 14.1. The chasm

We normally look at innovating as an *external,* objective process and refer to it with a view to managing it. Could we take a corresponding perspective *from within,* whereby the inner setting of individuals is what makes innovation happen?

### 14.1.1. *Business school*

The classical school of thought separates macro- from micro-levels. Well-established in economics, it has also led firms to specialize in their staff.

There used to be a time – for instance, in the 1970s – when IBM trusted its 120 high-profile planners to think of the next product lines, each in his or her own business domain. They were each locked in safe rooms and were continuously amassing enormous amount of data and information about their own ongoing business, from which they drew intelligence about the next phases. At the same time, thousand of developers and implementers focused on the nitty gritty level of operations.

The division of labor is no new thing. But it has percolated the granularity levels too: those who think big and those who think small.

## 14.1.2. *Apple*

Jobs was a well-known template for crossing the macro-, meso- (the middle level where we find our neighborhoods) and micro-levels at any rate. Possibly in the future, scholars will find that, in order to understand Steve Jobs, they had better study quantum physics. Why is this so?

First, because he navigated his firm and markets by zooming in and zooming out incessantly. Finding resemblance in micro details and macro-visions: as above, so below. His mind was not the mind of a Westerner only. In his youth, he was attracted to oriental thinking and made his way to India in search for wisdom. He did not find it there, but he gradually developed a dual approach from within: a left brain hemispheric view for analysis and a right hemispheric glance for synthetic vision. All in one, about anything, anytime.

## 14.2. Developing the chasm

Tracing back to history, we find similar traits in a few characters. One of them was Leonardo Da Vinci. Strange parallels can be found in Jobs' and Da Vinci's lives. They were both vegetarians, one was an abandoned child, the other was an illegitimate child. Leonardo was both an artist and a scientist. A most creative mind and an acute engineer. He usually wrote from right to left, and it has been suggested he was left-handed. Jobs declared himself ambidextrous (as suggested by example in an interview with Newsweek in 1984[1]), indirectly recognizing the symmetric activation of brain hemispheres in his staff too. Of all the peculiar traits, Leonardo and Jobs indeed have much in common. They are:

1) *Hemispheric balance.* Both are inveterate innovators who decisively blend art *and* science in one single human quest. Their brain seems to equally solicit their two hemispheres. Leonardo's mirror writing echoes the cross-hemispheric linkage of the cerebellum, whose "brain organ" seems to play an eminent role in blending rational and creative ways of thinking. Present research attributes heavy importance to the interrelations between the two hemispheres. Like Leonardo, Jobs made no separation between engineering and artistic work, and wanted his engineers to be creative as artists are. Recognition of this artistic talent is exemplified by the story of him insisting that the Macintosh team signatures be present inside the first Macintosh (see: http://www.vintagecomputing.com/index.php/archives/391).

2) *Varying Observer–Subject distance.* Acute observers of their times who were never drawn into the surrounding background noise *and, at the same time,* went to unsought productive depths with intense passion.

---

1 http://www.thedailybeast.com/articles/2011/10/06/steve-jobs-1984-access-magazine-interview.html.

3) *Thinking transdisciplinarily.* No domain is out of reach per se. A method from within helps in crossing established boundaries and capturing the essence of what lies beyond. Audacious thinkers, shameless players and incorrigible forerunners.

4) *Quantum behavior.* A living ecosystem that evolves by generating its own future.

We have studied Leonardo at length over the past few years [COR, 10], and could notice a "Leonardo method". Three common features among others stand out are:

– capable of working on a series of projects concurrently, and finding a unifying framework, not a division of his own time and energy;

– an ability to simplify to the quintessence after due observation;

– a genuine capacity to meaningfully link up apparently independent observations.

The above denotes an unleashed systemic thinking. When Jobs repeats his well-known *"connecting the dots"* mantra, we visualize Leonardo glaring at birds to invent the helicopter and so on. Countless examples are found in both biographies. Leonardo did not hesitate to dissect corpses in order to draw better models for his design from biology. Moreover, this was seriously heretic activity during his time.

A famous artist who connected the dots in special ways was Maurits Cornelis Escher. He customarily designed spaces that loop onto themselves, thus creating scenes where things become circular, instead of remaining linear as per a traditional depiction. No past and no future, just a universe where "things are instantaneous". And this exactly expresses one basic quantum property. By working linearly, we presuppose a total order on things, hence past then future. But here, everything we do modifies the future. You bring your ecosystem with you in the change. And this is what we see with Apple: only one perduring ecosystem that renews onto itself.

Look at Apple product interfaces: they do not contain things that are ordered linearly (take e.g. iTunes). The interface that you are given understands the general concepts far better, which guide you toward a pseudo-linear action. Not a side instruction manual, but your own desire. In doing so, the interface contains no slowing content, no thinking brake.

Someone who spans not less than personal computers, animation films, the music industry, smartphones, tablets, retail stores and digital publication by: (1) systematically reinventing a fresh identity for each of them, and (2) connecting them seamlessly into giant ecosystems, is the mark of an adventurous systemic mind. How many core products churns an Apple? Less than 10 (iMacs, MacBooks, iPhones, iPods, iTunes (and Store), Apple Store, App Store and OS X. Each is a leader on its own. How many mature paintings made a Leonardo? Arguably less than ten. Each being top of the line...five centuries later. Both in subject matter and in the fabric, including the technology used.

Yet, the drawings, the sketches and the blueprints are innumerable for each. As Jony Ive, Job's sister soul for design, once said *"we would be ashamed to say how many prototypes we make"* before a product.

In a nutshell: to understand Apple, scrutinize Steve Jobs. And to understand Jobs, investigate Leonardo Da Vinci. Appendix 3 provides an original and thorough analysis of the way the Maestro thought and worked. We believe this becomes of key importance for inventing new ways of doing business in the next future.

# You Said Reality? Which Reality?

*"Reality leaves a lot to the imagination."*
John Lennon

## 15.1. The chasm

Reality distortion field (or RDF), has long captured attention about a mesmerizing Steve Jobs. Bending the understanding of "reality" in the face of others. Albert Einstein said *"Reality is an illusion, although a persistent one."*

To think is to observe. What is the difference, if any, between a thinker and his/her thoughts? What if we can overlap the two?

Communication is a language. Considerable research has long shown that language and thought are quite entangled.

A linear thinking dominates our business world. Quite often, thinking is but a mechanical manifestation of a dualistic logic: right or wrong, good or bad, certain or doubtful, agreement or disagreement, etc. And this is a trap where entrenched positions tend to be then defended forever. This leads to dominate designs, which are arrangements that industry seeks to organize itself and perdure. For a breakthrough innovator, a dominant design at best bounds creativity and at worst blocks it. The "enemy" is not the competitor to beat, it is the dominant design to break! A whole new way of considering business, competition, and societal progress.

Is duality, then, not to be overcome? But how?

To communicate effectively requires choosing the right arguments, the right frequency that is suited to convince others. We impose our thoughts. An alternative would be to create a dialogue based on listening, a method that may remind us the Ancient Greek philosophers. And one issue is *how do you stimulate creativity among others?*

Leonardo Da Vinci elaborated a specific painting technique that brings about a sense of haziness, as if tones were "in between" known intensities. Indeed, the *sfumato* technique was his way to shift reality and induce subtle feelings in the observer who immediately experiences a distortion of plain evident facts and embarks into a distorted consciousness zone when glancing at the painting. The *sfumato* technique exploits peripheral vision by mixing colors and hues. It has been copied but never with the same level of expertise as demonstrated by the Gioconda painting. Does this technique not remind us of the so-called RDF ability of convincing which Jobs employed in the face of objections from peers and staff?

Influencing your staff means first understanding their reality and seeking ways to alter it. For such an ability, you need a dose of flexibility in retaining various points of view. Your goal is to reach the production of common meaning.

### 15.1.1. *Business school*

You think and you communicate your thinking. But communication is done in a duality. Players have a tendency to play rigid positions, and argue in favor of one camp, justifiably their own.

Brainstorm and do creativity sessions: *innovation is, before anything else, creativity.*

### 15.1.2. *Apple*

A surprising Leonardo Da Vinci was known to master the most advanced communication techniques. François I, King of France, *"appointed him 'First Painter, Engineer and Architect to the King', but also master of festivities. A legendary director and designer of prodigious special effects, the king's protégé did indeed have a talent for dazzling an audience, according to many eye-witness accounts"* says a comprehensive exhibition brochure [MAR]. In France, and particularly at Le Clos Lucé in Amboise, Leonardo da Vinci designed and arranged magical shows and extraordinary spectacles, becoming a master in the art of special effects. As a result he became the grand organiser of royal festivities. Thus altering reality and inducing virtualities.

With respect to the status of reality, Steve Jobs was also a pastmaster in the art of communicating. He did not envisage reality as we customarily do. His early days attraction to Eastern and Indian philosophy, as well as his works on a number of occasions denoted a penchant for seeking alternate realities instead. Detached from ambient noise, ambient thinking and saying "no" to usual common ways of seeing things. *Innovation is to say "no" to things.*

Jobs warped reality. To do so, he escaped duality – the confrontation of opposite arguments – and eliminated the communication pollution brought about by egos. His arguments are "vertical", not "horizontal". By this we mean that they fall down from above with unique intensity.

In so doing, he developed a thought modulator whose process can be described as follows:

1) To gather to an observation and exhibit it. Appendix 3 details the science of observation demonstrated by Leonardo Da Vinci and establishes similarities with Jobs. Such observation amounts to intense, systemic and repeated thinking. Evidencing the observations is the root of the next step.

2) To produce a collective meaning. Jobs does this by soliciting his staff, which enables him to provide feedback. Feedback is what produces consciousness, in this case collective consciousness. The observation becomes shared meaning. In C-K design innovation theory terms (see Appendix 4), this is acquiring a common knowledge base K. This knowledge *de facto* becomes shared knowledge from which to build a new, usually crazy, concept that *disjuncts* from the K base. He forces out a new way of seeing reality. This action alone shows signs of a genuine innovation act.

3) He qualifies the new concepts, imprints it on others' consciousness as *the thing* to look at and leaves his staff figuring out *how to expand it* in order to find workable and implementable solutions.

In so doing, Jobs followed a typical C-K way, as did Leonardo Da Vinci. Appendix 4 explains the steps in more details. By changing the perception of reality, Jobs was capable of changing people and this is what he did repeatedly, inside the firm and outside with partners and the world. Even the market *perceived* a new world upon the introduction of say, the iPod, or the iPad, or services like iTunes, to name only a few instances. An iPod was much more than a product. It was a fresh new behavior that allowed me to carry a thousand songs in my pocket, my songs, and to listen any of them at will, in any environment and so on, with the rest of Apple's products since the iMac.

Apple does not make products but generates meaning. By changing the perceived meaning, you change people, you change the world. A stupid product brings no meaning. A new meaning must be brought by a new product.

This also explains why Jobs went away from focus groups: these tend to restore the dominant designs through dual exchanges. The thinking line becomes "horizontally discussed", it may develop into opposed views, perhaps to be resolved by majority rules.

## 15.2. Developing the chasm

With respect to the status of reality, Apple is not a regular enterprise. It is first a thinking machine. It aims at perceiving the future from the weak signals observable today from the world and connecting them. Furthermore, its thinking is a collective process which generates a sort of global way of thinking.

Engage engineers as designers to generate new meanings in concept generation. The meaning of a product induces a profound psychological and cultural reason why people use a product. A question is *"where is meaning niched in products"*. The original meaning resulting from such design-driven research is often compromised when handed-over during concept generation (Dell'Era *et al.*, 2011, cited by [FAB 15]).

*"Engage engineers as designers to generate new meanings in concept generation"*; *"What is an effective marker event of radical innovation of meaning in concept generation?"* [FAB 15]. These authors answer by pointing to significant bridges between functional innovation and design-driven innovation.

When Apple engineers and designers experiment a multitude of versions of the same prototype, it is not for the purpose of entertaining dualities. Like Leonardo routinely did with his plentiful versions of a same functional drawing, as an example, it is for experimenting, that is confronting with the 3D reality of operating machines. For instance, to factually determine which version brings better user satisfaction, simpler operation, or lesser spurious steps, etc.

So, it is about connecting all pieces of experience in one understanding. The surprise comes from previously unseen corrections. Yet, brainstorming and other classical creativity techniques (Six Hats, Delphi, etc.) leave you with ideas. Problem is that people do not know what to do with more ideas. Everybody is full of ideas (at least they are at birth). Avoid doing too much (in many directions). Concentrate on important things.

Apple's thinking process goes around both brain hemispheres (left: analytical; right: global) and transcends them by initial intuitions that preempt the whole process (Figure 15.1).

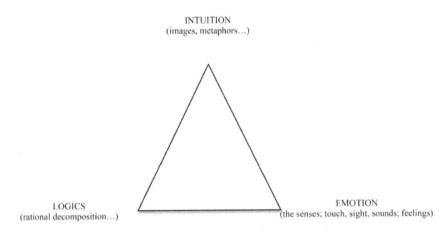

INTUITION
(images, metaphors…)

LOGICS
(rational decomposition…)

EMOTION
(the senses; touch, sight, sounds; feelings)

**Figure 15.1.** *Escaping from dualistic views requires a ternary model*

The above discussion tends towards become holistic. Leonardo Da Vinci had a remarkable humanistic stance in everything he was thinking, even if he designed incredible war and damaging machines. But, as both artist and inventor, his thinking was an integrated thinking, on Nature, on Man, and about art. The same as Erasmus before him, or Montaigne after, and many others. As a matter of fact, like Jobs, as we begin to understand the biography of the latter better.

A further development might implicate some notions of quantum mechanics. Here, an observer and the thing observed are the same thing. This leads to the notion of (quantum) entanglement whereby two distant elements form a unique *system.* This is yet a further understanding of Job's motto "connecting the dots." Jobs instantaneously perceived the world in a holistic way.

Have you yet noticed that the Apple ecosystem of products (and services and processes) constitutes a whole system? Most probably you already have. Yet, have you ever noticed that the ecosystem behaves as a hologram? In the words, any device therein, can light up, in essence (of course not in functions) the whole ecosystem?

Take one piece of software, say the iBooks author. As you learn by using it, you begin to notice that many features are working the same in, say, pages and so on.

What you learn here, serves your there. Nothing is lost on your learning path: each piece of software opens your mind to others, as if it were containing them.

Apple, a holographic company? We believe so, and that is why it foretells a future way of entrepreneurship. By not accumulating myriads of products, of services, of processes in our everyday life – often confronting and consuming themselves. By creating and encapsulating a myriad of new services within an amazingly limited number of products. The future value of business is meaning and Apple has already shown it to us.

In Figure 15.2, we show a diagrammatic view of how the traditional way of doing business leads to fragmenting it, while a holistic approach regenerates the global dimension. It may also explain why the Apple ecosystem is not primarily open to other heterogeneous elements.

We tend to think that Jobs, in as much as Leonardo Da Vinci, developed a sensory experience of the world that freed itself, and to a high extend, from the bias of the dominant thinking of their times. That they are born five centuries apart and the technologies have vastly evolved is no objection to that. For Steve Jobs may well prefigure, as a new Leonardo himself, a future way to envisage both technology and commerce, processes and engineering, and philosophy and consciousness as Leonardo did by then, in his notebooks [RIC 98].

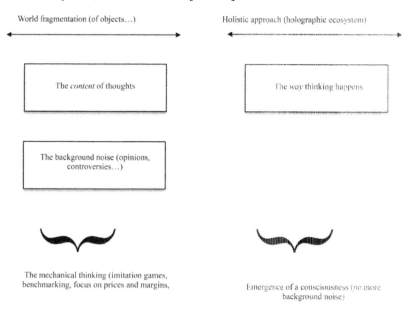

**Figure 15.2.** *Antagonizing classical and holistic modes of thinking*

*Learning never exhausts the mind* said a Leonardo who can be well-echoed by Jobs reportedly always learning all his life. The extreme perfectionism of both personalities is well-known. In its new History magazine, National Geographic [NAT 15] beautifully illustrates the X-ray vision about minuscule details of Leonardo, and at the same time his global method of thinking (thinking not shouting). Who can say less of Jobs' way?

Both designed *artifacts,* and in psychology, an artifact is an artificial psychic fact that probing consciousness may bring about. Jobs has more *knowledge bandwidth* than his peers have, or, better, less filtering out than what cultural conditioning lets in others' consciousnesses. A trait that allows the forging of *"crazy"* concepts apparently out of the blue, beyond market expectations and market segments beliefs. This stifles the classical market analysis approaches when doing radical innovation, as we have expounded in Part 1 of this book.

Hence, Jobs is literally a sensory magician. Yet, by consistently pursuing the tracks he envisioned (against all odds), he shaped a molded reality that followers embraced (and others despised). The Apple way is one possibility for molding worlds, there perhaps exist others bringing different technologies and products. Yet, Jobs *über alles* contribution might have been to open ourselves to a field of multidimensional possibilities.

It seems that a person who lived "with Windows" for 20 years sees the world quite differently than another who one day resolutely embraced OS X. For, again, the *experience* is different.

## 15.3. It's all about perception

After all, this is the story of perception. Perception roots our lives. Perception is everything and everything is perception. Here (Figure 15.3) is a systemic diagram expounded by Gérard Gigand [GIG 15] for the root concept of perception. Commenting on it requires the help of the methodology introduced in Appendix 5. For the purpose of his chapter, we project three reflections of the word:

– *About incompleteness.* First, any perception, a partial phenomenon is intrinsically limited by its unavoidable dead angle or limits to its observation. Hence the word *"abridgment"* to express this first partiality.

– *About self-referentiality.* Second, any perception is subjective. It is prone to auto-persuasion, appropriation and implication. Hence the word *"bias"* to denote this second partiality.

*– About indeterminacy.* Third, perception can be considered as a selection, a focusing, or leads to circumscribe. Hence using the word *"fragmentary"* to convey this third partiality.

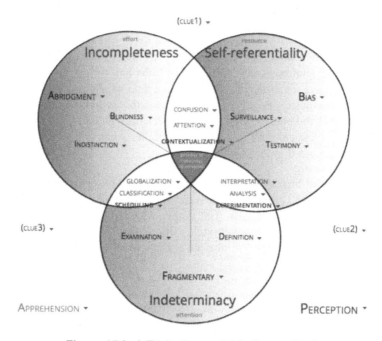

**Figure 15.3.** *A Trialectics model for "perception"*

Beyond the cross-influences of the three new words (not detailed here), the process ends up by having the three "including thirds":

– "contextualization" at the action level,

– "experimentation" at the attitude level,

– "scheduling" at the management (adaptation) level.

This expresses the genuine process of any perception. It is clear Jobs played all three and simultaneously, which seems a rare feature. One anecdote is revealing. One day, to make the observation (perception) that the internal iPhone design could still be improved, Jobs provoked a self-evident test *(experimentation)*. He barely plunged one model into water (organization of the observation, hence *scheduling*) just to make his engineers conspicuously aware of the lost and available free space inside, as revealed by the bubbles gradually rising *(contextualization)*. What an appealing lesson, through a mediating perception (hence the synthesis: *apprehension*). What a management lesson, and a motivating force: what would you do then, as an engineer, if not turn your back on any fear, being struck by the evidence of a situation?

# Combining the Genes

## 16.1. Taking stock of a flat list of genes

Throughout this book, it appeared that Apple had very much acquired a deeper thinking about business. We begin by gathering the genes, in view of first making a summary. Appendix 1 provides the list of acquired genes. Here it is for convenience.

Gene *AAPL001 – Accept risk, turn it into opportunity.*

*If you do not accept risk, then keep away from any business.*

Gene *AAPL002 – Have Chuztpah.*

*Excellence in management requires Chutzpah.*

Gene *AAPL003 – Product is more than product.*

*The design team's objective is to come up with an "insanely great" product.*

Gene *AAPL004 – Turn essentials inside out.*

*Removing what is unnecessary is more valuable than blindly stacking functionality.*

Gene *AAPL005 – Product existence is by using it.*

*Enhancing customer experience rather than the spec sheet.*

Gene *AAPL006 – Always keep the end in sight.*

*Polarize all developments by working toward an aim.*

Gene *AAPL007 – Be your own judge.*

*The best approach to come up with an "insanely great" product for designers is to realize the product they would have liked to buy.*

*Gene AAPL008 – Impose strategic rhythm to markets.*

> *Do not become a "me-too" supplier. Anything you launch should be strategic.*

*Gene AAPL009 – Aim for the top.*

> *By thinking from the top, you let others consolidate your basis – from below.*

*Gene AAPL010 – Anticipate.*

> *A lower position can no longer be overcome through frontal assault on the same battleground, rather by skating where the puck is going to be.*

*Gene AAPL011 – Select your fights.*

> *This strategy requires patience, as the puck may move slowly.*

*Gene AAPL012 – See the new in the old.*

> *A new category is formed out of blurring the divisions between old ones.*

*Gene AAPL013 – Practice perseverance.*

> *Success requires perseverance. Not to be confused with stubbornness.*

*Gene AAPL014 – Failure today breeds tomorrow's success.*

> *Recognizing a failure is a tough act for a leader. Arguably, it is the only way to make progress.*

*Gene AAPL015 – R&D is a means, not an end.*

> *The product roadmap drives the entire R&D effort.*

*Gene AAPL016 – Decouple R&D spending from innovation spending.*

> *Technology change management includes an acquisition policy which must outrun competitors.*

*Gene AAPL017 – Acquire the right company at the right time.*

> *Technology change management includes an acquisition policy which must outrun the competitors.*

*Gene AAPL018 – Software is a powerful force.*

> *Software pushes other technology types around; therefore balances power within enterprises.*

*Gene AAPL019 – Software differentiates.*

> *Regard software as a differentiating factor, not as a commodity.*

*Gene AAPL020 – Software is different development.*

> *Software development presents a fundamental management issue. A modern manager must understand software specificities.*

*Gene AAPL021 – Respect software status and software people.*

> *Good software cannot be built on top of software that people hold in contempt.*

*Gene AAPL022 –Software process.*

*Mastering the software development process is not in contradiction with hiring exceptional, off-the-scale talent.*

*Gene AAPL023 – Reveal markets indirectly.*

> *Use that terrible failure as bait revealing "truer market".*

*Gene AAPL024 – A good idea requires the right timing.*

> *Bad timing does not imply a bad idea. A good idea must wait until the time comes for it.*

*Gene AAPL025 – Blend form and function.*

*As a medium is a message, a form factor carries meaning, but it should be aligned with content, i.e. function.*

*Gene AAPL026 – Meaning is everything.*

> *A form factor that is not balanced with function relegated to decoration.*

*Gene AAPL027 – Top management must take charge in consumer markets.*

*In the consumer goods market – whatever the size – top level management is the front line when it comes to products.*

**Table 16.1.** *The acquired list of genes*

When analyzing the above list, we can observe two recurrent characteristics: Apple breaks the classical notions of competing and innovating.

– *Evolving competition.* The depolarization from the classical views about competition. It all seems as if Apple had mastered an art of escaping the dualism inherent in fighting competition. In fact, it does not fight competitors as if they were enemies. It opens new strategic market spaces and even appears to turn its back on competition. It actually repolarizes competition by offering it a new vision, on which it sooner or later embarks (because of the lure of profit to be made in these new markets). But with a supreme differentiating factor: it establishes a value gap and solidly maintains it. In conclusion, Apple has evolved the notion of competition by stirring it from a leading position.

– *Evolving innovation.* In the innovation game, it is not R&D that opens the way. It is a combination of vision, market opportunities, and technology, plus a capacity to extract all the juice from their connection. It is a multidimensional approach.

Let us recall the table issues at beginning of Part 1 in a more synthetic way. By matching the nine topical domains of interest which made up Part 1 with the above two synthetic characteristics, we obtain the following:

| Topical domain of gapping interest (and the underpinning key business issue) | Higher relevance to innovation capability | Higher relevance to competitive capability |
|---|---|---|
| Risk taking (uncertainty) | Yes | Yes |
| Product design (products) | Yes | – |
| Market studies (markets) | – | Yes |
| Giving up some fights (competition) | – | Yes |
| Entering new markets (leadership) | – | Yes |
| Apple, the learning company (skills and talents) | Yes | – |
| On R&D | Yes | – |
| On company acquisition (external growth) | Yes | Yes |
| Managing software development (software versus hardware) | Yes | Yes |

**Table 16.2.** *Relevance to the two synthetic characteristics of innovation and competitiveness*

Which translates into the following table, which represents the knowledge base:

| What relates more to innovation | What relates more to competition | What equally relates to both |
|---|---|---|
| Product design | Market studies | Risk-taking |
| Skills and talents | Competitive fights | Company acquisition |
| R&D | Entering new markets | Managing software/hardware |

**Table 16.3.** *The root knowledge base. Each cell contains a wealth of knowledge, both traditional (e.g. business schools) and Apple-made*

## 16.2. Setting the stage toward a combined dynamics

By attempting to summarize the traditional thinking in competitiveness – in other words searching for the dominant designs found in the notion of *competitiveness* first, and *"innovativeness"* second, we will gradually proceed toward a genuine synthesis of the genes. For this, we use the design methodology based on C-K theory (see Appendix 3 for an example).

### 16.2.1. *In search for dominant designs*

To begin with, what is in a dominant design (DD)? A DD is relative to the way a given business domain of activity is organized and reflects the accumulated habits of the sector. It expresses the credos which all players abide by: the modes of operating, of competing, of innovating, etc. Often they take the form of dogmas, as the inception moments which originated a given dominant design have been lost, being likely undocumented and sometimes belonging to a previous generation of workers.

By looking at the gene list, we detect two immediate dominant designs pertaining to *competitiveness:*

C-DD1: *"Competing in dualistic environments."*

This DD is a way to signify face to face competing by differentiating and specializing. A traditional view which business schools have long propagated.

C-DD2: *"Growing dimensionally."*

This DD expresses the predominant of growth in either size, product line (diversification of the products catalog) or market volumes (which may translate into market shares). Another traditional view which business schools have long advocated, across the firms spectrum from startups to giant corporations.

The same effort will be made for "*innovativeness*":

*I-DD1: "Innovating within one's core business."*

This DD expresses the coring on the business sectors in which a firm is already established. The rationale is evident: to stabilize a business position and take up arms for competition with a clear edge.

*I-DD2: "Innovating within one's core competencies."*

This DD expresses the capitalizing on the firm's inner best assets. Indeed, traditional views advise exploiting the accumulated skills. The rationale behind says that a firm competes well only where it is best at.

There are many more dominant designs at work in any established business field, as these grow and mature. For the sake of simplicity and brevity, we only focus on the above and process our methodology forward.

### 16.2.2. Breaking the dominant designs

To open up new avenues of innovation, we break the rule nested in each above dominant design. Which leads to defining breaking axes for the four DDs found above:

| *C-BR1: "Escaping duality."* |
| --- |

This axis is an obvious translation of the first dominant design.

| *C-BR2: "Escaping monodimensionality."* |
| --- |

This axis focuses on combining blending several growth directions at once.

| *I-BR1: "Widening core business."* |
| --- |

This axis is an immediate rephrasing of the corresponding dominant design.

| *I-BR2: "Acquiring dynamic competencies."* |
| --- |

This axis targets the capacity to *evolve* skills and talents, competencies and know-how. Not to carry them over through time necessarily, a sort of accumulation or sedimentation of competencies (hence the breaking effect searched), but instead to refresh them according to the needs (of market, of industry, whatever).

At this stage, we don't try to validate the above expressions: these are "crazy" directions for entering straight unknown zones. The breaking axes assert directions without knowing if they may be feasible or not.

### 16.2.3. *Blueprinting radical "crazy" concepts*

It is now time to formulate a few working expressions in the form of undecidable root concepts C0 in order to satisfactorily operate C-K theory. These can be reformulating the breaking axes defined above. As an example:

| |
|---|
| *C01: "Acquiring competitiveness beyond core assets."* |

| |
|---|
| *C02: "Evolving 'innovativeness' beyond 2D models."* |

We will briefly develop these two concepts through a simplified C-K diagram. The end purpose is to obtain "formulas" that can be taken by third organizations as a quintessence of an Apple DNA. These formulas are meant to be replicable and adaptable to target business contexts. There will not be an estimation of the possible cost of adoption for internalizing the resulting formulas as cultural projects within a firm as this falls beyond the scope of this book. Nor is there an attempt, and for the same reason, in developing deeper and wider C-K diagrams.

We only show here a few ideas for food not to make the discussion too heavy. The C-K diagrams can be developed much further in the same line; here only the first expansions and a few main findings are shown. We believe it is enough for the clear enough understanding of the approach.

A C-K diagram shows the technique of expansion performed in the conceptual space C (left in the diagram) from the initial knowledge base in the K space (right in the diagram). Remember that the knowledge base is primarily formed by Part 1 and Part 2 of this book and supplemented by the total relevantly accumulated knowledge (the latter which of course is developed elsewhere, e.g. in books and university or professional trainings of all sorts). It is dubbed to be the sum of "business school knowledge" and "Apple knowledge" since it was drawn from discussing nine basic thematic domains of business activity, both "*à-la-traditional-business schools*" and "*à-la-Apple*".

A more detailed discussion of the process, which may sometimes result delicate, is offered in Appendix 3. Please refer to this background material, and the specific references attached therein, for any desired further investigation.

# 17

# Evolving Competition

This chapter works on the notion of competition (and competitiveness) by evolving it. We use C-K theory for designing the C01 blueprint concept found in Chapter 16:

> C01: *"Acquiring competitiveness beyond core assets."*

## 17.1. Cracking open the notion of "competition"

Two complementary angles of using Trialectics are (i) a more foundational understanding (Figure 17.1) and (ii) a more routine view that resembles everyday use (Figure 17.2[1]). The first angle will supply an in-depth study of an "Apple way" of competing.

In Figure 17.2, the notion of competition involves friction-based duality (greed: complicity and challenge), the uncertainty of the results (contest: analogy and desire) and the actual distinction in the works (resemblance: acquisition and redundancy). The three "including thirds" reveal the *resources* needed for action, the posture in exposure (*advertising*) and the indispensable adaptation to *markets.*

---

1 Diagram obtained with the support of G. Gigand [GIG 15].

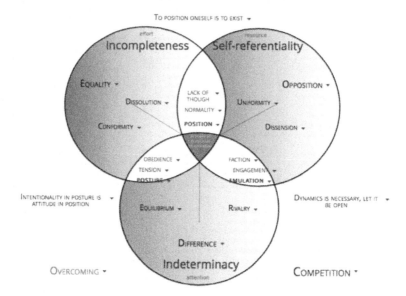

**Figure 17.1.** *The Trialectics diagram working out the concept "competition" ontologically*

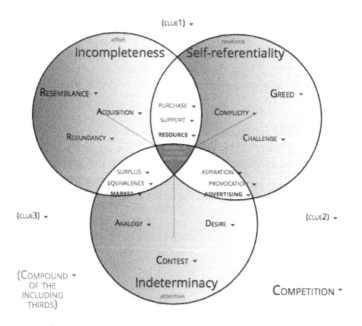

**Figure 17.2.** *Two Trialectics diagrams working out the more mundane concept of "competition"*

## 17.2. Designing an expanded understanding "competition"

We now base a C-K development on the above diagrams and start from a fundamental declaration from Steve Jobs, in that building Apple was a far more difficult endeavor than designing products for Apple. The point in this legacy nugget is not the products and services catalog; it's the company behind them and the capacity of the latter to churn them out correctly. Jobs strikingly distinguished the big capacity shift:

– from innovation *results* (1st level), to;

– innovation *process* (2nd level) to;

– innovation *capacity* (3rd level).

There exists an order of magnitude in difficulty from each level to the next [COR 15]. What Jobs worked at during his span at the company was to build the company, which is today symbolized by a brand. It therefore makes sense to start understanding what "competition" means for Apple by first "exploding" the concept of brand. This has been provided using Trialectics in Appendix 5.

Let's interpret the findings for "brand" (Figure 17.3) – they are called the "including thirds":

– vocation: in between "structuration" and "utopia";

– creativity: in between "norm" and "exemplar";

– authority: in between "distinction" and "cohabitation".

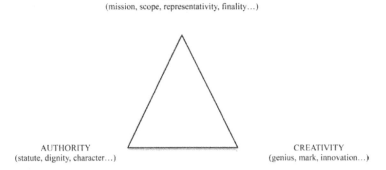

VOCATION
(mission, scope, representativity, finality...)

AUTHORITY
(statute, dignity, character...)

CREATIVITY
(genius, mark, innovation...)

**Figure 17.3.** *The ontological triangle of any brand*

The conceptual expansion of each of these three root terms by a C-K diagram should be done in a powerful way first before deepening the roots. The reason why we use the three "including thirds" is that they, by construction, offer the maximum expansion power to the initial concept of "competition" while remaining entirely faithful to it.

Indeed, Jobs wanted his brand to exercise the maximum differentiation through a more singular brand.

C-K development goes through radical expansions in the C concepts space (Figure 17.4 shows a simplified example). The main finding can then be formulated as a set of second generation concepts as follows. In the example given:

– *inducing customer behavior: engagement, faction*;

– *creating a unique customer and user experience (commensal)*;

– *stirring imagination to the limit (both utopia and structure)*.

This may be synthesized as:

> Formula AAPL-C: "Compete against your own self (emulation) by polarizing a posture."

The formula evokes and results in a notion of overall internal tension that underpins the way competition is handled.

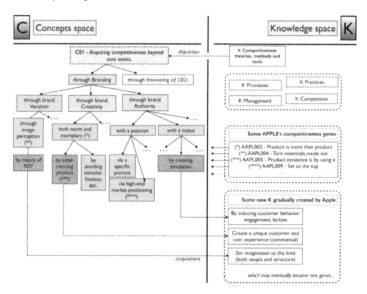

**Figure 17.4.** *An example of a C-K diagram expanding the notion of "competitiveness" from the acquired knowledge of Apple genes. Such development can be performed further on, here is shown in a simplified view*

# 18

# Evolving Innovation

This chapter is complementary to the previous chapter. It works on the notion of innovation (and innovativeness, or the capacity to innovate [COR 15]) by evolving it. We use C-K theory to design the C02 blueprint concept found in Chapter 16:

> *C02: "Evolving 'innovativeness' beyond 2D models."*

## 18.1. Cracking open the notion of "innovation"

Two complementary directions of using Trialectics are, again, (i) a routine view that resembles everyday use (Figure 18.1) and (ii) a more foundational understanding (Figure 18.2[1]).

Innovation can be seen phenomenologically as the process (Figure 18.1) of reconfiguration of an existing (i.e. perceived) situation, with a degree of impact. This leads to *adaptation* (as the including notion between *continuity* and *method*), *tension* (as the notion reuniting *interpretation* and *abandon*), and *incrementation* (as the view unifying *routine* and *personalization*).

Figure 18.1 develops the concept of innovation from a more mundane standpoint. Innovating on sometimes mean:

– resourced out of a mainstream: *deviance* is the attractor of self-referentiality, which has *conquest* and *improvement* as agents;

---

1 Diagram obtained with the support of G. Gigand [GIG 15].

– installing a yet unknown degree of change: *transformation* is the attractor of indeterminacy, which has *propagation* and *distance* as agents;

– pursuing a diffusion effort: *dissemination* is the attractor of incompleteness, which has *assimilation* and *reference* as agents.

The notion of *effervescence* emerges between assimilation and conquest, as it means the necessary buzz around innovating. *Mutation* appears between improvement and distance and suggests the reaching of a no-return point at some stage. *Influence* between reference and propagation signals the limits of a measure of an innovation adoption process.

Figure 18.2 supplies a more in-depth view of an "Apple way" of innovating. A similar analysis leads us to perceive that innovation is a tensed quest for "*what's beyond*" in an open way. And it is based on processes (Apple uses many processes), while the outside world sees reconfiguration and impact. The kernel formula is written as:

*Adaptation – Tension – Incrementation*

The next chapter will develop these findings as the firm's signature, where everything appears to be on eternal move upwards and nothing can be stagnant. Every step, aligned with the gradient path, produces an irresistible innovation capacity.

## 18.2. Designing an expanded understanding of "innovation"

The C-K design process works by expanding an undecidable concept further. To start expansions in a most powerful way, we use the Trialectics diagrams of Figures 18.1 and 18.2.

The main finding can be formulated as a set of second generation concepts as follows:

– processes geared toward anticipation;

– co-evolving customer ecosystem systemically;

– stirring imagination to the limit (both utopia and structure);

– setting the stage for evolving environments (inside, customers);

– providing purpose and implication to customers.

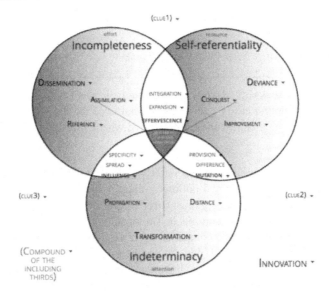

**Figure 18.1.** *The Trialectics diagram working out the concept "Innovation" routinely*

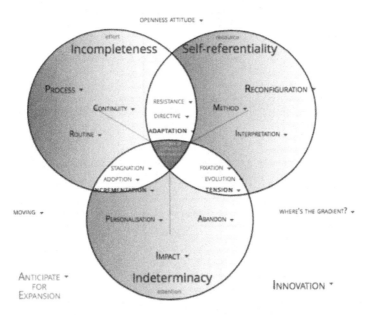

**Figure 18.2.** *The Trialectics diagram working out the concept "Innovation" ontologically*

This may be synthesized as:

> **Formula AAPL-I:** *"Keep open the hard[2] (gradient) way by sliding to a few new opportunities"*

Every time it seeks to make a breakthrough, it seems that Apple chooses the hardest path and not an easier path. This is what is called the *gradient path*, i.e. the path which bears the most ascending derivative when considering the continuum on *markets*.

Innovating and competing are so intertwined within the fabric of Apple that it becomes hard to separate the two notions. Actually, the gradient curve is the liaison path between them: first designing surprisingly novel strategic market space categories that nobody has ventured in (innovation gradient is gapping markets), then reaping the benefits while competition gathers momentum around it. While the basic mechanism is not at all new in industry, it is its periodic reinstatement (frequency of change) that sets a maximum, and arguably yet unmatched, power.

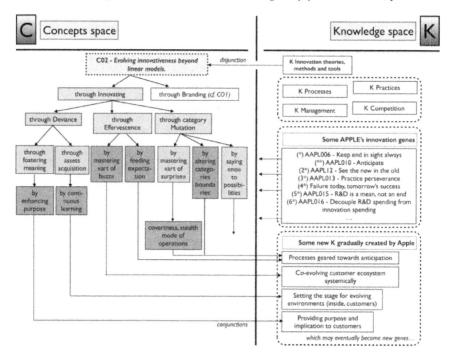

**Figure 18.3.** *The C-K diagram for C02 on Apple way to innovation*

---

2 Readers familiar with Frank Zappa will recognize here a reference to "Broadway the Hard Way" Frank Zappa's album.

This certainly confers the most difficult path to copy for competitors. When we think that often competition works by "gravity", i.e. by ascending to what a previous entrant has done, we see the sourcing for cycle long gaps, both technologically and market wise, where the law of growing returns work for as long as feasible.

# 19

# A Company Under (Dynamic) Tension

Apple always strives to: (i) anticipate, (ii) align its operations and culture along with an anticipated idea and (iii) stick to the anticipated idea until it yields the (big) returns it always unmistakably expects.

Anticipation is evidently seen in targeting new strategic markets, but also in acquiring, then growing, the competencies needed in the more or less distant future. It is a multidimensional approach.

## 19.1. Tension is a co-evolving dynamic

Apple is a company under constant tension. It is this tension that aligns it with big ecosystems that has helped it to nurture and grow. It is that very tension that provides the underpinning meaning that seeds any of its actions. The tension is coherence in alignment and completeness in action (Figure 19.1).

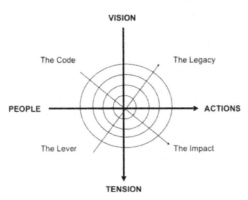

**Figure 19.1.** *The generalized MagicEye diagram as a cultural pattern scheme*

At Apple, it is seen at all levels (extracted from [COR 08b]):

– *objectives* are not merely "objectives"; their apprehension leads to time-based vision, i.e. the end aim. And *management* installs tension, which is capaciting the vision of the aim. This is the *power* axis;

– while management aims at stretching the alignment with the vision, it routinely works at monitoring the rapport between teams (*people*) and tasks (*actions*). However, people reach their accomplishment by consideration of the aims and the executive directions that are set for them. Then four interplays appear that signify the dynamic rapports between the four basic generalized notions. This is the *lifeline* axis;

– people embody the vision through an explicit system that we call a *code*. The code is clothed with varied names in specialized fields. It can be the reference cooking book from a visionary chef, a business plan from a new entrepreneur or the guiding textbook for students. In the case of Apple it comes from adherence to the vision. Vision stirs people's energy as an invisible manager. The resulting effect of putting the code into use is termed *impact*. This measures the potential effectiveness of the code. Together, these two secondary notions form the *method axis*. A suitable method – the particular way to work something out – can free man from tedious trial and error. An experiment without a method is at best silly and at worst evil. The genuine power of a method is to transcend natural man's abilities. We have detailed Da Vinci's codes – his working approach – as the most relevant role model that could be found;

– the right ingredients to focus upon in order to realize the vision are called the *lever*. All actions are performed through a kind of chemistry that is not amenable to a mere code. The code plus the lever can stir and project what people inherently have.. Steve Jobs seeded and accrued that historical lever role and embodied it into the people's minds, then the Apple University. That is his true legacy, which serves as a model reference for all. What ensues is the development of a reference (the meaning of a model result) that finds its true place – i.e. its significance – in the target social group. We call this "testimony" the *legacy*. This is the *significance* axis: the degree of meaningfulness of a given cultural pattern scheme to its authors or stakeholders. A scheme without meaning is useless and it is meaning that establishes entire societies (and firms, organizations, including the greater information and knowledge society).

These are four power lines that combine in the synthetic diagram as depicted in Figure 19.1.

## 19.2. Tension is a dynamic toward futures

The main challenge of any organization resides in providing the link between present and future. It is fundamentally a sustainability issue.

The four axes described are "futures axes" and yet they help in reinstalling a present to which the project can be identified to. They do this by relinquishing any projective action that would detach from a genuine interaction with the present. The transformation of the present is the real work that brings transformation and evolution.

The MagicEye diagram helps to signal whether the project takes up the challenge to be pointed in the right direction. If a future exists, it must (potentially) exist in the present otherwise it remains an idea. Because the *linear* continuity of time is merely an illusion that creates past–present–future alignments, it is our view that not anchoring on the present leads to depleted futures. Therefore, the MagicEye diagram exacerbates a relationship between structural time evolution and the notion of present. Does a future exist outside the mind of the one who thinks there is one? We believe not. Linear thinking and sequential models have long invaded our cultures and, unavoidably, inoculated our minds and impacted our inability to "see" things. But the decision-making process is about *constantly resolving the tension between the present and its potentialities*, even before looking at the consequences. The constant reinterpretation of possibilities transcends the linear models and calls for a new way of perceiving "future". In a nutshell, Figure 19.1 unfolds the present, *from* the present *to* the future.

With Apple, the connecting-the-dots approach (a backcasting approach) reverses a *possible future* back into its generating process (the seeds of becoming). Apple is a constantly evolving firm, regenerating itself through the interplay of the eight factors of the MagicEye.

Thus, the dynamic reinterpretation of the present onto itself supports:

– *global and leveled foresight*: addressing multiple levels and their correspondences from personal/local to global level. This is a "think local and act global" approach poster that crosses the micro and macro frontiers. The whole idea with Apple University is to ensure a coherent an actionable meso level in between;

– *organic dynamics*: enhancing interrelationships and their dynamics. This installs a systemic behavior which enables evolution from present. The forming of interrelations induces a complex becoming that deeply serves the firm at first and impacts its ecosystem in the sense of complexity sciences. It elaborates adaptive behaviors.

Armed with such tooling, Apple can support a new art of change by smoothing out purely classical hierarchical management, as well as the traditional business process reengineering, total quality management, focus groups, etc. methods. It operates not on notional analysis phases, but on methods (and processes) of becoming. A *company of becoming*, how can it not be thinking the future? With it, the future starts *now*.

### 19.3. Walking the way

This book approaches Apple's singularity in unique ways. We first observed the facts, including the amazing successes and first-rate failures that were revealing in that matter.

We then called on history and made stunning parallels with Da Vinci, the genius man of the Renaissance who, alone, made ample way for a flurry of innovations, which remained largely impossible to even think for his fellows at his time. Today, his way of thinking behind the scenes is still mostly uncovered as the scholarly and artistic focus is still positioned on the known artifacts. It contributed in clarifying a number of useful threads at method level.

At first, the parallels drawn with Steve Jobs were totally unexpected, until his capacity to churn out innovations in a multidimensional way came to our attention. Don't be deceived: the parallel goes deeper and further. It isn't much the result that counts but the *way to do* things.

This is a forbearing result for the competitive firms of recent years: firms change the way you think, with a rigorous method that they exercise systematically, and produce without *a priori* limits! *Stay foolish, stay hungry...*

It was only due to the power of C-K theory that inner traits of an Apple's method could be excavated. We were fortunate to be able to use it in our own consultancy for years beforehand. For the intrinsic multidimensionality aspects, Trialectics was found to provide far reaching global pictures of the two concepts of competitiveness and innovation.

At this stage, an *Apple way* boasts signs that resort more to quantum universes than Newtonian spaces. They may deserve to be developed further as quantum laws slowly seem to take over our globalized ways of doing business, of living and of interrelating.

As we attempt to integrate the above, the image of a rainbow comes to mind, and it reminds us of the long-forgotten old rainbow Apple Computer logo, bearing the same symbolic meaning.

# Overcoming Common Blocking Points

> *"Reality leaves a lot to the imagination."*
> John Lennon

Why is it that, after almost four decades, no other company as specific as Apple seems to exist? Have we still not learned how to churn out several of those super-innovating and super-competing firms? After all, top-notch innovators are not such a rare breed... are they? Or are there more obstacles than we expected which prevent us from having them?

The previous chapters have attempted to evidence those "nuggets" or genes that appear to underpin the advent of such a company. But what are the obstacles along the way? This chapter attempts to highlight a few of them.

## 20.1. The need for an innovation molecule

Most firms have learned to work *in* innovation, which means they strive to produce advanced results, or sometimes avail themselves of some innovation process that leads to such results. Apple seems to work *on* innovation:

1) by permanently seeking the gradient path in lieu of *a priori* innovative results – this grants a formidable anticipation capacity;

2) by subordinating its catalog to this gradient process. This happens by stepwise incrementing the intermediary prototypes long before they are plunged in the market;

3) by capitalizing on the impressive gap created as a result, which entails being careful not cannibalizing previous gaps, hence refraining from changing the rules too often.

This builds a metaprocess that agglomerates the genes into an irresistible innovation molecule, We have not seen quite as often such disposition in our client base at any time (Figure 20.1). And far less for a longer period of time. The mastery that is required behind this metaprocess sets a company at top level in maturity scale.

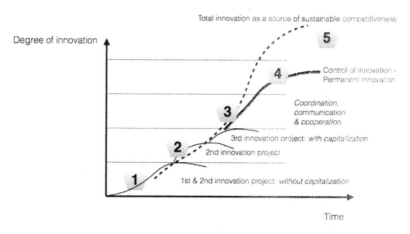

**Figure 20.1.** *Innovating through merely sequencing projects does not necessarily yield an optimized bottom progress line [COR 15]*

*In our previous book, Innovation Capability Maturity Model [COR 15], five levels of maturity are being distinguished:*

1) *Initial.* An initial product development project (no knowledge capitalization is made).

2) *Repeated.* A series of innovative projects makes little capitalization. Trials and errors dominate the development.

3) *Coordinated.* Projects are coordinated between themselves. With a mutualization of the corresponding accumulated knowledge. A new strategic dimension appears: the progressive integration of what innovating entails in the enterprise.

4) *Managed.* All that pertains to innovating is integrated within different departments. An innovation policy appears and the innovation activity is managed.

5) *Sustained.* Innovating is embedded in the firm's culture. Methods and tools (including processes) are evolved to strive over time.

In [COR 15], we observed the roller-coaster path of Apple's historical phases across these levels and noticed it took Jobs many years before aggregating the genes into a coherent whole that established his company at level 5 (Figure 20.2). The result so far has been cohesive innovation capacity and the ultimate aggregative embodiment obtained is its cohesive brand. Actually it is a *whole brand*, created from all possible interactions.

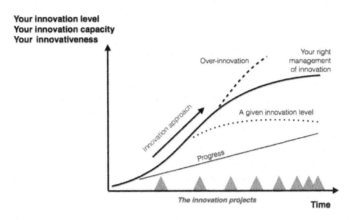

**Figure 20.2.** *When innovating is the essence of the firm's culture, all methods and tools serve it and warrant best competitiveness over time, sustainably [COR 15]*

## 20.2. A need to revisit risk-taking

An innovation molecule is like a restless engine. As we have seen for Leonardo Da Vinci, its indigenous aspiration is to re-interpret a different world every once in a while, for each of us. Actualizing it, however, requires overcoming one single barrier in the background: a repeated capacity to take risks. In Part 1, Chapter 2 showed more a personal attitude toward risk-taking. Let us take another contrastive look at a term that casts hazard, venture and chance, all at a same time.

The following two tables take risk-taking as a subject matter and expand the associated meaning in order to formulate actionable propositions. Methods for expanding the understanding include: singling out the relevant *dominant business designs*, mobilizing the associated knowledge, breaking them by delineating the *rupture axes*, charting the resulting *innovation fields*, etc. Applying C-K theory works them thoroughly. Table 20.1 is more indicative of a conservative view on risk-taking, while Table 20.2 expounds what Apple has been up to.

In our consultancy, when coaching start-ups, incubating companies and mentoring novel young and less young entrepreneurs and executives, a natural tendency to shield from risk was frequently observed – a possible reason is that risk was perceived as an *outside* factor – hence the multiplication of market studies to create confidence. The point is whether the entrepreneur has sincere *gut feelings*: the venture and possibility come just from within, where he/she knows…instantly. It is the *meaning* within us that inspires our productions and makes us move; and it is impossible to cheat with it. It is the meaning consistently spoken about through this book: with the Arts/Science of Leonardo, within the genes, built in the products, etc. Famous consultant Stephen Covey says it in a few words: "*Motivation is a fire from within. If someone else tries to light that fire under you, chances are it will burn very briefly*".

Students graduating from business schools, engineering schools and universities share the same, perhaps inherited, feeling about risk. Could we instead advise business schools with a quantum approach to risk-taking: a whole new domain of coaching where intuition and inner guidance, assurance and visualization of the desired aims aligns the forces within and sets an outward stage for realization? This would unite Eastern with Western culture, arts and science in the Leonardo sense, and benefit the economy at large.

The early Apple employee Guy Kawasaki, already quoted in the introduction, stated: "The best reason to start an organization is to make meaning – to create a product or service to make the world a better place".

Combining technology and liberal arts was a leitmotiv for Steve Jobs. Here is a citation relating to Apple's philosophy at an special event held by in March 2011:

> "*I've said this before, but I thought it was worth repeating: it's in Apple's DNA that technology alone is not enough. That it's technology married with liberal arts, married with the humanities, that yields us the result that makes our heart sing and nowhere is that more true than in these post-PC devices. And a lot of folks in this tablet market are rushing in and they're looking at this as the next PC. The hardware and software are done by different companies. They're talking about speeds and feeds just like they did with PCs. Our experiences and every bone in your body says that that is not the right approach to this – that these are post-PC devices that need to be even easier to use than the PC. They need to be even more intuitive than a PC and where the software and the hardware and the applications need to intertwine in an even more seamless way than they do on a PC. And we think we're on the right track with this, we think we have the right architecture not just in silicon, but in the organization to build these kinds of products. And so I think we stand a pretty good chance of being pretty competitive in this market and I hope that what you've seen today gives you a good feel for that*".

| RISK-TAKING - classical view | What it is at business schools | Where are the dominant designs | What are the consequences |
|---|---|---|---|
| Avoiding risk | Model risk in math formula | The future becomes predictable, an entanglement of the possibilities | We learn to see the world as it shall be seen |
| Shielding attitudes | Perform market surveys, analysis and the rest of it to ensure competition is well analized – Build (cross-)equity to stabilize ecosystems | The future is already (statistically) seen in rear-mirrors sold by external consultants | The world is seen as uncertain all around |
| Protection from change | Raise barriers to entry | Delegation of own firm ability to external fixtures | Needs quick responses, stressing |
| Management disincentives | Organize forum and discussion groups | The couple (product, competency) loses energy | Innovation must be pushed, forced – staff works in "assisted" mode |

**Table 20.1.** *Analyzing risk-taking in the form of transferable knowledge (the classical view)*

| RISK-TAKING - Apple's view | What it is for Apple and others | Where lies a new lineage | What are the consequences |
|---|---|---|---|
| An ad-venture, once in a lifetime | A value proposition for Apple, an out space gadget for the observer, arrogance for the examiners | What hasn't been done isn't impossible | All things are seen equal: no *a priori*, equal readiness in the face if unknown things |
| Test, experiment, again and again | Buying the future at the expense of sweat | Promising paths emerge from all around | The Unknown drives the seeking of opportunities |
| Lineages | From iPod to… | Periodical evolutions of each product, creating value each time | Coverage of entire areas - competition is self-excluded |
| Inner drive pulls the strings | A thirsty attitude, a knowledge-hungry behavior, a disruptive mentality: | Opportunities for everybody create space for everybody | Innovation expands - Innovation culture grows endogenously, thus can be evolved |

**Table 20.2.** *Analyzing risk-taking in the form of transferable knowledge (Apple's view)*

*"Once it's been done, it's done – you know."*
John Lennon

# Conclusion

Malibu Police Chief: *"You don't draw shit, Lebowski. Now we got a nice, quiet little beach community here, and I aim to keep it nice and quiet. So let me make something plain. I don't like you sucking around, bothering our citizens, Lebowski. I don't like your jerk-off name. I don't like your jerk-off face. I don't like your jerk-off behavior, and I don't like you, jerk-off. Do I make myself clear?"*

The Dude: [after a pause]
*"I'm sorry, I wasn't listening."*
The Big Lebowski, 1998

**Figure 1.** *The most iconic Apple's rainbow logo, as designed by graphic designer Rob Janoff. It was in use over the years 1976–1998 (source: http://www.edibleapple.com/2009/04/20/the-evolution-and-history-of-the-apple-logo/)*

In Silicon Valley, bleeding edge technological capacity and business rivalry are deeply entrenched with a common goal: success.

Despite this, Apple has nurtured a mode, a way of its own, which speaks of something else. This something else would not negate the technology acumen or the managerial poise that dominates there and in many places of the post-modern world – and, should we say, by far.

This "something else" is *Apple's way of thinking and striving*, and it often departs from traditional thinking, the thinking that is still taught at many business schools. This book has gradually elicited a number of threads that seem to form the DNA of that company. We have weaved them and shown that they amount to reinvent the two notions of competitiveness and "innovativeness" in surprising ways.

A good friend of ours, a brilliant engineer who became a human factors specialist (ergonomist) by vocation, one day confessed that it was somewhat paradoxical for him to remind students that (apart from rare exceptions) humans have two knees, a characteristic that seems frequently forgotten by the people designing workplaces for people in seated position.

A manager should remind his employees that, in any consumer goods products market, the fundamental objective is to design the best possible products, the most beautiful and easiest to use, and to make sure, through permanent customer satisfaction monitoring, that these objectives are reached, keeping in mind that "[the rest] *will be given to you as well*" (Matthew 6:33)[1].

A reader who has only read the genes chapter, and who would have never heard of Apple, may well ask himself why such obvious considerations deserve a book.

As humans, we are easily distracted by pursuing too many objectives, which is the most certain way to forget the essential.

We currently live in a troubled period, where the news flow, even in countries considered as developed, is made up of a hopeless list of hate, injustice and violence in all forms. The quest for beauty, common to Leonardo Da Vinci and Steve Jobs, may appear in this respect as a futile concern of rich men. We believe this is not the case. Any human being looks for, needs and deserves some kind of beauty, down to

---

1 Matthew 6:33 New International Version (NIV) "*But seek first his kingdom and his righteousness, and all these things will be given to you as well*" https://www.biblegateway.com/passage/?search=Matthew+6%3A33&version=NIV.

every aspect of his life, not necessarily the technological ones, but also including food presentation, clothing, etc.

Jobs has installed what resembles a DNA ladder for reaching new heights, where before him there was none. The ladder is shaped as a helix, a double helix. In fact, when embracing life in a multidimensional way, each lives a nonlinear path. We believe Job's major legacy has been to equip Apple with a self-programmable tomorrow. An engine propelling it into the 21st Century. Apple thus stands beyond linearity. A non-surprising offspring would, for instance, be a "programmable computer", using human thought, for instance, and varying the functions set.

We would like to think that the comparisons we've made between Leonardo Da Vinci and Steve Jobs as individuals also extends to their respective periods of time, Steve Jobs announcing a new Renaissance of modern times to come, just like Leonardo Da Vinci did for the one we know from history, ending the dark medieval times. Apple instead builds holograms: the whole is available from any angle. All in all it is a difference in thinking.

The Apple Way, in short, is nothing more than concentrating on the essential, and forgetting about the rest, which will come anyway in due time, as a necessary fill up of what was correctly seeded once.

The question is now *"who can grow and guard Apple's DNA?"*. And this is more important than the price of gas ... because it perpetually seeds new orders. A coherent 1% of new genes are more powerful than the 99% past ones.

Altogether, the plain and simple content of this book has been proven to be worth about one trillion dollars. Wouldn't you like to gain even a small portion of this?

> *"There are two basic motivating forces: fear and love. When we are afraid, we pull back from life. When we are in love, we open to all that life has to offer with passion, excitement, and acceptance. We need to learn to love ourselves first, in all our glory and our imperfections. If we cannot love ourselves, we cannot fully open to our ability to love others or our potential to create. Evolution and all hopes for a better world rest in the fearlessness and open-hearted vision of people who embrace life."*

> John Lennon

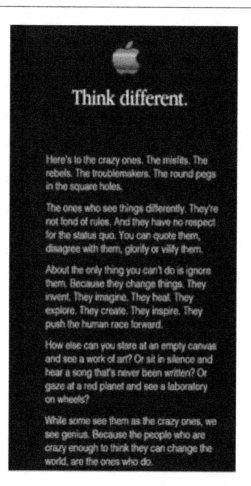

**Figure 2.** *The original "Think Different" motto that served in the famous Apple's 1984 advertisement*

# APPENDICES

*"It'll be okay in the end. If it's not okay, it's not the end."*

John Lennon

In the following appendices, the reader will find relevant and useful complements for exploring *Apple's Way, The Hard Way* further.

# Appendix 1

## Apple Genes List

The 27 genes discussed in this book are recapitulated here:

*Gene **AAPL001** – Accept risk, turn it into opportunity*.

> *If you do not accept risk, then keep away from any business.*

*Gene **AAPL002** – Have Chuztpah.*

> *Excellence in management requires Chutzpah.*

*Gene **AAPL003** – Product is more than product.*

> *The design team's objective is to come up with an "insanely great" product.*

*Gene **AAPL004** – Turn essentials inside out.*

> *Removing what is unnecessary is more valuable than blindly stacking functionality.*

*Gene **AAPL005** – Product existence is by using it.*

> *Enhancing customer experience rather than the spec. sheet.*

*Gene **AAPL006** – Always keep the end in sight.*

> *Polarize all developments by working toward an aim.*

*Gene **AAPL007** – Be your own judge.*

> *The best approach to come up with an "insanely great" product for designers is to realize the product they would have liked to buy.*

*Gene **AAPL008** – Impose strategic rhythm to markets.*

> *Do not become a "me-too" supplier. Anything you launch should be strategic.*

*Gene **AAPL009** – Aim for the top.*

> *By thinking from the top, you let others consolidate your basis – from below.*

*Gene **AAPL010** – Anticipate.*

> *A lower position can no longer be overcome through frontal assault on same battleground, rather by skating where the puck is going to be.*

*Gene AAPL011 – Select your fights.*

> This strategy requires patience, as the puck may move slowly.

*Gene AAPL012 – See the new in the old.*

> A new category is formed out of blurring the divisions between old ones.

*Gene AAPL013 – Practice perseverance.*

> Success requires perseverance. Not to be confused with stubborness.

*Gene AAPL014 – Failure today breeds tomorrow's success.*

> Recognizing a failure is a tough act for a leader. Arguably it is the only way to make progress.

*Gene AAPL015 – R&D is a means, not an end.*

> The product roadmap drives the entire R&D effort.

*Gene AAPL016 – Decouple R&D spending from innovation spending.*

> Technology change management includes an acquisition policy which must outrun competitors.

*Gene AAPL017 – Acquire the right company at the right time.*

> Technology change management includes an acquisition policy which must outrun the competitors.

*Gene AAPL018 – Software is a powerful force.*

> Software pushes other technology types around; therefore balances power within enterprises.

*Gene AAPL019 – Software differentiates.*

> Regard software as a differentiating factor, not as a commodity.

*Gene AAPL020 – Software is different development.*

> Software development presents a fundamental management issue. A modern manager must understand software specificities.

*Gene AAPL021 – Respect software status and software people.*

> Good software cannot be built on top of contempt software.

*Gene AAPL022 – Software process.*

> Mastering the software development process is not in contradiction with hiring exceptional, off-the-scale talent.

*Gene AAPL023 – Reveal markets indirectly.*

> Use that terrible failure as bait revealing the "truer market."

*Gene AAPL024 – A good idea requires the right timing.*

> Bad timing does not imply a bad idea. A good idea must wait until the time comes for it.

*Gene AAPL025 – Blend form and function.*

> As a medium is a message, a form factor carries meaning. But it should be aligned with content, i.e. function.

*Gene AAPL026 – **Meaning is everything.***

> *A form factor that is not balanced with function relegated to decoration.*

*Gene AAPL027 – **Top management must take charge in consumer markets.***

> *In the consumer good markets – whatever the size – top level management is the front line when it comes to products.*

# Appendix 2

## On the True Nature of Software

This appendix provides the basic elements necessary to understand the specificities, and hence, power of software, as a distinctive activity requiring consideration, management and metrics.

### A2.1. Software role, software people role

A washing machine, a car radio or almost any product of everyday life now incorporates some amount of software (often a lot). This software is frequently "buried", in the sense that its presence is not obvious or "visible", neither for the end-user nor even for the manager responsible for its development.

In many cases, softwares have creeped into long-lived products – frequently through the man–machine interface – without any noticeable change in the development process.

As time goes by, software development costs demonstrate that software is no longer negligible, but rather may even become the main product.

However, the technical hierarchy within the enterprise remains unchanged. If, for example, the company makes electronic products, the electronics specialists will still occupy all management positions, with no intention of granting software people the smallest part of their influence. A similar situation occurs when other engineering specialities are historically dominant in the design process: hydraulics, mechanics, etc.

Even in companies already confronted with several coexisting engineering disciplines (such as mechanics and electronics, biology and computing or material sciences and chemistry), and therefore, we would think, its better to be prepared for change, software will always be considered as something "apart", as we had the opportunity to observe throughout enduring professional experience.

The under-representation of software specialists, in places where decisions are taken, unavoidably leads to poor decisions, whether from a technical or managerial standpoint:

– *Technical* given the increasing capabilities of programmed solutions which make them good candidates to replace other technologies, and refusing to evolve in this direction is a sign of a product which will be rapidly made obsolete by other, more innovative competitors.

In the business of home regulation systems or temperature measurement devices, long established and powerful players, like Honeywell or Siemens, feel the push of totally new players, of a much smaller size (for example the French startup Netatmo), without any previous presence in the domain, but with products designed to be seamlessly integrated in iOS or Android ecosystems. With the Internet of Things, a massive trend in this direction is underway.

– *Managerial* because a company that doesn't manage to give software people the decision power, in line with their importance with respect to the product, falls into the traps described above.

Software activities are always the last ones to perform. They are indeed impacted by any last minute change made in the hardware first, of which material embodiment they depend for final tests and verifications. Due to this dependency, software people are often under scrutiny from top level management and held responsible for any delay.

Of course, just like any other contributors, they have their share of responsibility. But it is well known that, in large multi-year projects, nobody will question a weeks delay in the early phases, whereas the top level management will require real time reporting for a single half day delay at the end. As it happens too often by that time, their concern will be to identify and punish the culprits (but not necessarily in this sequence), or to suggest false good ideas (such as parallelization up to a ridiculous and counterproductive extent).

In companies where managers have a poor software culture, it is very easy for the non-software contributors to place the blame for delays on software people shoulders, and thereby ruin their reputation.

On the other hand, companies with a good understanding of software issues not only perform well for software, but also take advantage of this knowledge to cross-fertilize other engineering disciplines. For example, software people are good at requirements management, because they are confronted with highly complex products in their line of work.

The expertise gained by software people in adopting a functional standpoint, and in managing and controlling the baselines of each and every associated requirement, is something extremely valuable for other disciplines, which, for historical reasons, are usually behind on these subjects.

The more advanced companies in space, aeronautics or automobile industries have developed a systems engineering discipline, adapted to large, multidisciplinary projects, wherein software appears as one technology among others. Despite this, they mostly fail to grant software people access to top level management.

## A2.2. Software, an immaterial product

### Software Project Tracking

*"The invisible part of everything that you thought you could see, you can't see."*

G.W. Bush (offering his appraisal of the Palestinian/Israeli situation, Interview with ITN, Crawford, Texas, Apr. 5, 2002)

Software is probably the only engineering discipline where the manager is unable to estimate the progress of work. In software, the well-known reply to the manager asking about work progress is *"90% finished"*, but can be stuck there for an indefinite period of time.

A software project in industrial conditions consists of managing thousands or, more likely, tens of thousands of artifacts (code, but also various documents, i.e. test procedures, test results, etc.), about which a "software illiterate" manager has no idea at all.

This quantity also rapidly increases with the level of quality required, being maximal for software critical software subject to particular requirements, or checked by independent authorities (EASA in Europe and FAA in the US for the aeronautics case). Of course, in this case, delays and costs explode, as compared with a "normal" development.

Industrial solutions exists to develop software with minimum bugs, but these are costly, even very costly, and, which is even worse, in a business where time to market is essential, they also require much more development time.

It could be argued that such considerations concerning critical software reside far away from Apple's business, but this could turn to be a short sighted view. What if Apple decided to move toward the automobile industry, with self-driving vehicles, subject to safety critical requirements regulations?

As a way to circumvent the difficulty he/she has to visualize work progress, an incompetent manager grasps the only thing which is accessible to him/her: *the mythical number of lines of code*. Unfortunately, this "metric" remains more delicate to use than it seems, is programming language dependent, and is in no obvious way correlated to the effort, nor to the work progress.

Generally speaking, sticking to effort estimation alone, only the *function points method* makes an estimation of the software development effort possible, independently of the coding language used. Unfortunately, it entails some expertise, and requires a detailed functional specification of the software product to be developed, which is beyond most organizations capability.

A manager relying on lines of codes monitoring to track and manage a project will go nowhere as nothing is easier than developing lines of code, especially with modern development methods. Of course, the question of whether these are necessary, and of required level of quality, is another story.

Indubitably, in the absence of other metrics, a rough estimate of the volume of code to be produced makes no harm. Because, at project launch, it is much better to know whether the final product will be in the range of thousands, or the tens of thousands, of lines of code.

As a result, a manager is unable to properly manage a software project without a good understanding of the very nature of the software activity. And no MBA will help the manager in this regard.

### Project planning

> "*Without music to decorate it, time is just a bunch of boring production deadlines or dates by which bills must be paid.*"

Frank Zappa

Project management, planning and scheduling, are now firmly established disciplines, based on a large set of good practices and knowledge, and this is not the place to recall them in detail.

Let us just go back to the basics. A "good" schedule is one obtained after all tasks have been identified (Work Breakdown Structure, or WBS), estimated (in effort first, and then in duration, given resources hypotheses), and later on nested one to another according to the sequencing (and possibly, parallelization) constraints. Dedicated software applications easily calculate the earliest delivery date possible, after all these elements are estimated and introduced.

If the resulting output isn't in line with the objective, hypotheses are modified but always in a forward calculation mode.

Needless to say, a backwards calculation mode, consisting of going back in time without any feasibility consideration, from the specified due date to the current time, is not a scheduling exercise, but nothing more than disguising the manager's fantasy into some fake reality. Of course, a manager can always twist the software project leader's arm, possibly using authority, but in this case putting him/herself beyond the notion of commitment, as a result of a negotiation; a hard one possibly, but nevertheless a negotiation.

All the foregoing about scheduling is true, whatever the domain considered. *The software specificity is that, if the manager exerts an unrealistic pressure on delays, he or she will get due value for money.* It is always possible to deliver a piece of software at any given point in time, but too early and it could be functionally incomplete, or poorly tested, or both.

We have no information on how Apple schedules its developments. We would need to wait for iPad or iPhone developers to write their memoirs to have some indication on this.

As briefly mentioned later, manager "Steve Jobs version 1.0" was not reputed to base his schedules on the virtuous approach described before.

However, a "Steve Jobs 2.0", and more generally Apple now, seemed to adopt a more realistic attitude on this topic.

Of course, the launch of the Maps Application (the Google Maps competitor) can be presented as a notable exception, but the trouble was more in the data than in the code itself, and mapping the entire planet surface, down to the smallest lane, isn't easy. Assuredly, the mistake was more in not positioning the first version as a Beta version, which was the only realistic possibility at that time.

This episode resulted in the departure of Scott Forstall (then Apple's iOS Senior Vice President). Even though other reasons probably explain his mistakes, successors are warned of what their fate will be in case their management leads to a similar failure.

This does not mean (and we come back to this later) that the Apple developers do not feel a huge pressure on their shoulders, but this does not go as far as requiring the impossible from them, without listening to what they say. That being said, in the present case, an irresponsible attitude, which characterizes a contempt of software people and software in general, can lead to nothing but disaster.

### A2.3. Software development activities – the CMM model

> *"If you don't know where you're going, you could wind up somewhere else."*

> Attributed to Yogi Berra,
> American baseball player

#### *The CMM model*

A manager without a software culture identifies software development as coding. This couldn't be further from the truth, as we will see through the CMM model developed by former IBM Vice President Watts Humphrey at Carnegie Mellon University-based SEI (Software Engineering Institute).

The capability maturity model (CMM), initially dedicated to software (or its SPICE, or software process improvement and capability determination (ISO/CEI 15504) equivalent), evolved into capability maturity model integration (CMMI), a more general model, extended to any engineering activity, including mechanics, electronics, etc.

In what follows, we will stick to the CMM model, because, although partly obsolete, it is simpler and dedicated to software, which makes it more suitable for our purpose.

Any organization developing software can be situated at one of the five levels of the CMM model, described hereafter. From the initial level 1 where most companies are, process improvement initiatives aim at reaching higher levels, and possibly the ultimate objective of level 5. This level is hard to reach but not impossible, and has been reached by a number of organizations (many of them in India).

### "Initial" (maturity level 1)

No company standard process exists at this level. Weaknesses are *not identified* and projects participants are not precisely informed of what is expected from them. Reaction to problems happen in panic mode, without a clear identification of priorities. Still, it may happen that, due to the exceptional talent and commitment of the project leader, some projects can be successful, but this is just a result of heroic behavior, which, on the long term, always leads to discouragement or burn out but rarely to the next level:

### "Managed" (maturity level 2)

Each project follows a disciplined approach, as *documented in several plans* (development plan, quality assurance plan, configuration management plan, etc.). At this level, it is the project leader's responsibility to define, apply and maintain the corresponding plans.

### "Defined" (maturity level 3)

At this level, a company-wide discipline is documented and applied, through a *standardization* and *inter-projects capitalization*. The project plans result from instantiating the generic plans. The developers are adequately trained.

### "Quantitatively managed" (maturity level 4)

Projects are managed on the basis of *quantitative measurable objectives*, related to both products and processes. The quality objectives expressed by the customer are translated into project objectives, and form the basis of the project planning.

### "Optimizing" (maturity level 5)

All processes (including the improvement process) are *predictable and quantitatively* managed.

At this level, which is a sort of developers nirvana, everything, absolutely everything, is planned and happens according to plan in absolute calm and serenity, without a need for the single hour of overtime[1].

---

1 The CMM model was recently redefined to suit the context of designing and managing innovation by [COR 15], thus leading to the Innovation Capability Maturity Model (ICMM).

This certainly isn't the working environment of the Macintosh team (see Andy Hertzfeld's book [HER 04]). Moreover, incompetent management prefer level 1 Brownian activities, which they assimilate to efficiency.

The structure of the CMM model distinguishes several key process areas, the 18 KPAs, associated with one of the five maturity levels of the model (Table A2.1).

| Maturity level | KPA | Code |
|---|---|---|
| 5 Optimizing | Defects prevention | DP |
| | Technology change management | TCM |
| | Process change management | PCM |
| 4 Quantitatively managed | Quantitative process management | QPM |
| | Software quality management | SQM |
| 3 Defined | Organization process focus | OPF |
| | Organization process definition | OPD |
| | Training program | TP |
| | Integrated software management | ISM |
| | Software products engineering | SPE |
| | Intergroup coordination | IC |
| | Peer reviews | PR |
| 2 Managed | Requirements management | RM |
| | Software project planning | SPP |
| | Project tracking oversight | PTO |
| | Software quality assurance | SQA |
| | Software configuration management | SCM |
| | Software subcontract management | SSM |
| 1 Initial | (none) | |

**Table A2.1.** *The 18 key process areas of the original CMM model*

Every key process area can be further developed into key practices and the level of implementation indicates whether the key process area can be considered as satisfied or not.

For example, requirements management (RM) includes 12, project planning (PP) has 25, etc. In total, 316 practices are associated with the 18 key process areas of the CMM model.

Reaching a given maturity level requires that all key process areas associated with this level are fully implemented.

The fact that no key process area is associated with level 1 does not mean that people at this level just do nothing. To the contrary, level 1 is characterized as hectic and inefficient because it can be disorganized.

Key process areas can be present at any maturity level. Even at level 1, it is possible to find practices related to defect prevention (DP), which is normally a level 5 key process area. Similarly, software quality assurance (SQA) does not, obviously, start at level 4.

What the model says is that it would be counterproductive to place the emphasis of the improvement efforts on key process areas which are not associated with the targeted level: this will come in due time.

Of course, nothing more than guesses can be made about the level of maturity of Apple development teams. Apple does not communicate on this.

It is unlikely that Apple has internally set software maturity objectives to reach, because companies reaching high levels of maturity do communicate on this, as a legitimate source for pride.

It can be, however, taken for granted that a manager at Apple is not remaining with eyes wide open when asked for resources to perform requirements management, configuration management, quality assurance, verification tasks, etc.

In a very remarkable way, and extremely shocking at first sight, it can be noticed that there is no such thing in the CMM model as a key process area, or even activity, related to coding.

From the model standpoint, this does not mean that the coding activity does not exist, but rather that it is not considered as a key one, on which it could be possible to distinguish a non-mature organization from a mature one, or which could be related to project failures.

Even though a manager may not subscribe to a software process improvement objective – after all, this is an own decision, and we will come back to it later – he must know and understand the particular nature of a software development, and a model like the CMM is suitable for it, as a sort of functional analysis of everything which has to be performed, irrespective of the particular development environment, or methodological choices, of the company.

### The mystery of the small, yet costly software fix

> *"Ces choses là sont rudes. Il faut, pour les comprendre, avoir fait des études". (Those things are tough; understanding them requires a degree)*

Victor Hugo
*La légende des siècles (1859)*

The following true story is a good illustration of the common misunderstandings of software, which is too frequent among managers.

Further to a problem of software origin encountered in the field, a software fix had been defined, likely as simple as modifying a few instructions in the code (sometimes one single instruction suffices). We may note this also happens frequently for problems without a software cause, but which can be fixed by software.

Everything being fine, the manager expected the fix to be implemented at once, and of course, at virtually no cost. In the end, he was unable to understand why the software teams in charge submitted him a substantial cost and delay estimation, if not an obvious lack of motivation on their side.

But this doesn't have to be the case. Unless authorizing dangerous and uncontrollable modifications on the spot, any software change must undergo a precise sequence of steps, impacting a considerable number of software artifacts, which have to be managed and controlled in a very specific way, not to mention the necessary verification and non-regression tests, etc.

With complex software, this cannot be just a one person task.

A manager who refuses to make the intellectual effort to understand this reality will have a hard time with his software teams. The loss of confidence will translate into conflicts, and possibly, subtle retaliation strategies from the software team.

Consultants trying to sell the "process message" had such a hard time that, since 2000, they now prefer to promote "agile" methodologies (including, for example, the SCRUM method). These methodologies complement, rather than contradict, the process approach, as they restrict their field to planning and implementing cycles of development (the iterations), without touching on the much more difficult issue of the programmers organization of work.

## A2.4. Software people productivity

*"The system is that there is no system. That doesn't mean we don't have process. Apple is a very disciplined company, and we have great processes. But that's not what it's about. Process makes you more efficient."*

Steve Jobs, *BusinessWeek*, Oct. 12, 2004

We once had the opportunity to discuss with a CEO employing software people, the concepts of maturity models, process capability, etc.

At this point, he expressed total skepticism toward the potential benefits of the concepts, preferring his own approach, of biblical simplicity. He said:

*Given the fact that variations of productivity among programmers can easily range on a 1 to 10 scale, firing the bad programmers and only retaining the best ones, brings a dramatic improvement to global productivity!*

The practical difficulty of implementing such a policy, in some environments, is not sufficient to disregard this idea without further analysis.

The statement concerning the productivity variations is not totally false, but it is first of all necessary to explicit the concept of productivity in this case, as well as going back to the root causes.

As already pointed out, productivity under the coding speed angle is meaningless, given the small weight of coding activity within the entire software effort.

In the 1980s, organizing competitions among programmers using different languages or development environments was a common practice, and it led to see which one would be the "fastest" guy. We have seen this in CAD-CAM shows, where the winner was the first programmer to produce the NC tape to machine a given part, defined through its drawing ("blueprint").

But more than a way of comparing CAD-CAM environments used, this competition was in fact highlighting the dexterity of the winner, his ability to read a drawing, etc.

The capacity to code fast does not appear to us as a very significant issue. However, it is true that some programmers have a distinctive talent, compared to their colleagues, to produce a code which is more easily readable, maintainable, testable, etc.

Process gurus struggle to admit this, as their approach is based on the premises that individuals can be easily substituted, with the same repeatable result, as long as the process is mastered.

Pushing the reasoning to the extreme would lead to fixing the exact same salary for all programmers, which is seldom seen, in practice. Some process ayatollahs go as far as describing a world wherein developers would just have to blindly stick to predefined job instructions, down to the smallest level of detail. Such a vision might possibly be useful in a mass production environment, but certainly not in design environments.

Software productivity discrepancies among individuals can be related, to some extent, to dissimilarities in levels of training or experience, but the explanation falls short of explaining everything.

Undeniably, some individuals are off the scale when it comes to programming, and are to software programming what Michelangelo is to painting or sculpture. We have previously mentioned Jean-Marie Hullot, hired by Steve Jobs, as an example of individual belonging to this very small "population".

# Appendix 3

# On Purposefully Recalling Leonardo Da Vinci Design Innovation Codes

*"Ideas are everywhere, but knowledge is rare."*

Thomas Sowell

This appendix provides a study of how Leonardo Da Vinci worked, based on numerous books about the Master, trips to the region of Vinci, in Tuscany, Italy, and discussions with referent scholars over the years 2006–2014. The specific references provided at the end account for these.

The purpose of this is to show an anterior instance of how a master of innovation routinely worked. Five centuries later, we find the many similarities with the ways of thinking of Steve Jobs striking. To understand Apple, Jobs is the key focus. And for knowing Jobs, Da Vinci remains the archetypal template.

The common methodology tool for harnessing the *way of the masters* is C-K theory from the theory of design innovation (*théorie de la conception innovante*) team of the Scientific Management Center (*Centre de Gestion Scientifique*, or CGS) at Mines ParisTech in Paris (Prof. A. Hatchuel, B. Weil and P. Le Masson). Our legitimacy in using C-K theory for the purpose of this book is our professional practice as associate practitioner with the CGS.

By associating Leonardo to a way of thinking and C-K theory, we establish a better documented groundwork which may help deepen studies about other *masters*. One of them is Steve Jobs, whose creative talent can be matched to similar features.

## A3.1. Introduction

In this section we illustrate the idea that the synthetic and integrated science and art of Leonardo Da Vinci may offer firsthand knowledge and inspiration to a designer and design theory field practitioner. From repeated observation first, then through the interplay of *arte*, *scienzia* and *fantasia* (creative imagination), his mind endlessly conceived.

This would merely resemble a typical scientific method yet to be developed through the later centuries, if it wasn't for his advocated emphasis on: augmenting *sperienza* (experience); abstracting imaginative concepts; relating them to chunks of knowledge in staggering numbers of dispersed fields; materializing them through engaging *demostrazioni* (embodiments); and consistently perfecting each of the above in whirling back and forth oscillations.

All these operations are meant to reveal functional relationships between various parts of an analyzed system with a view to elicit theoretical models: he created both knowledge complexity and understanding by way of systemic thinking. The aim of this section is to contribute to a more communicable and universal elucidation of the way Leonardo thinks with the deepest benefits for our post-modern times.

## A3.2. Where a Leonardo inventor and designer shows the C-K way

It remains an enigmatic thing to explain how a human appearing in a non-scientific and non-technological century could come up with so much of a legacy covering both engineering and arts, encompassing virtually all then known disciplines, at a perfected level, and seemingly instantly. How can a single individual, with a few handfuls of paintings and, barely a couple of sculptures, attain such erected heights in art?

"*I can't believe such a man could have ever existed*" exclaimed King François I after the death of Leonardo Da Vinci (1452–1519). Yet, up to today, "*most authors have looked at* [his work] *through Newtonian lenses, and I believe this has often prevented them from understanding its essential nature*" [CAP 07]. Indeed, an estimated more than 300 inventive wonders are attributed to him in an amazing number of domains of human endeavor, amounting to a staggering kaleidoscope of human experience. By contrast, scholars do not seem to have yet elucidated his "method"; as for contents, even his wide mathematical work, is still not yet documented properly. In a previous publication [COR 10], we showed how the Leonardo legacy work can impact education and research in innovation; here, we straightforwardly twin his approach with design thinking.

The approximately 6,000 surviving pages from his notebooks lay a protean collection of knowledge islands. To the naive observer, they offer a seemingly disorganized set of sparse information. Not so in Leonardo's mind: *"his science gave him a coherent, unifying picture of natural phenomena"* and *"shows why it cannot be understood without his art, nor his art without his science"*. Wouldn't this convey a glimpse into complexity theory and system theory?

For Leonardo, painting and engineering became a *discorso mentale* (mental discourse). To know how something worked was not enough, he also needed to know why. He also emphasized that this understanding was a continuing intellectual process. Therefore, painting was considered an intellectual endeavor. "The scientific and true principles of painting are understood by the mind alone without manual operations" said Leonardo, inviting us to a theory of painting residing in the conceiving mind.

Our purpose is to take a posture "orthogonal" to his productions: what was, if any, Leonardo's way? What made him so successful equally in quality and variety? We acknowledge that Leonardo was natively multidimensional in his way of thinking, being also capable to visualize and transform with astounding capacity complex worlds into the meager material embodiments only feasible then. While we attempt to shed some light on such a multidimensional process, we repeatedly observe the uncanny experimental resemblance with the methodical application of the C-K theory to practical situations.

## C-K theory in a nutshell (or: a posthumous Da Vinci reference point)

> *"He who loves practice without theory is like the sailor who boards ship without a rudder and compass and never knows where he may cast."*

As an abstracted design reasoning process, C-K theory is a powerful approach for discussing design phenomena. Design is here intended as creative engineering, including new functional spaces, requirements, competencies, business models, etc. It's an activity that spans industrial design, architecture, science, and usage at least [HAT 10] and enables to make a radical and definitive distinction between what's uncertain (resorts to probabilities) and what's unknown (resorts to logics).

C-K theory establishes a formal distinction between a space of "concepts" (C) and a space of "knowledge" (K) as a condition for design:

– the K-space is populated with propositions that possess a logical status. Which means that *"matching experts"*, i.e. individuals having relevant expertise or knowledge, are able to evaluate them. It is gradually augmented and continuously (re-)organized, through mobilizing theories, practices, crafts, traditions, tests, verifications, validations, etc. – all of which can be dubbed knowledge. K looks like a collection of categorized islands of identifiable subspaces;

– the C-space contains propositions always bearing undecidable status: otherwise a concept gets by definition thrown back to the K space.

To start a design process, an initial element is formulated through a blueprint proposition in a way that can be dubbed "undecidable": hence it belongs to the concepts space. To trigger the design process, the blueprint gets progressively refined by successively adjoining attributes and this constitutes the basic C-K expansion process. Hence, the C space is unfolded through a tree structure(s) while the concepts are progressively adjoined attributes. Note that the attributes can only come from K, even the initial blueprint can only be forged by using known words!

An unbounded process expansion creates "design images": progressive concepts growing a series of attributes. The obvious question is how to systematically dig an unknown space? Modeling the dynamics of design goes by expanding the space of concepts and the space of knowledge concurrently. Four operators, C→K, K→C, C→C, and K→K, compose what can be imaged as a "design square" (Figure A3.1) and their interplay captures the variety of design situations.

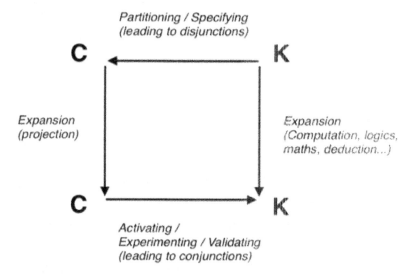

*Partitioning / Specifying*
*(leading to disjunctions)*

C ←———— K

*Expansion*
*(projection)*

*Expansion*
*(Computation, logics, maths, deduction...)*

C ————→ K

*Activating /*
*Experimenting / Validating*
*(leading to conjunctions)*

**Figure A3.1.** *The design square is the "connect-the-dots" engine. It evidences four generic operators working backwards and inside. Together, will implement the design activity. For designers, the K→C disjunctive operator reads: "disconnecting from the Known", while the C→K conjunctive operator reads: "connecting to a known element"*

*Relevance to Da Vinci practice methodology*

C-K theory practice seems relevant in Da Vinci's methodological context for at least three reasons:

1) It organizes a rational and constructive way of designing unknown desired "objects". For Leonardo, object categories have names paintings, sculptures, machines and mechanics, anatomy, geometry, maps, guidelines, etc., and his progressive way is no less rational.

2) It returns the trace of the design steps – a genuine design intelligence as it sets a capacity notion rather that gets stuck into the effects – the target results. Here dwells a quintessence of innovation maturity. Leonardo remarkably understood this point as his work is an ongoing dance drawing on skill, creativity, and knowledge, by equally and constantly interplaying them.

3) It rests upon the able practitioner – not the scientist - the practical task to conceive things. Likewise, Leonardo insisted on his engineering designs being busy with execution skills.

## A3.3. Create by starting from an empty space, then connect the dots

How do you innovate? The problem-solving way? An example is the Branch-and-Bound algorithm. You can navigate a tree and find the right leaf, the optimum solution, which already exists. To innovate is to get a new leaf, but how do you do that? In the B&B algorithm, it's an empty space. That's where you've got to start any breakthrough you can think of.

This was the starting point for A. Hatchuel when inventing C-K theory. The following sections explains how he did it.

*How to start from an empty space?*

Express an undecidable proposition (can't prove "true" or "false") and separate the world into two spaces: K (existing and missing knowledge, where propositions have a logical status), C (concepts, where propositions have no logical status).

*What the C-K approach means*

Implementing C-K theory:

– sets a clear departure from classical creativity methods and techniques, e.g. brainstorming or six hats techniques, or Delphi-based methods. Also a transcending departure from problem finding/solving approaches and other reasoning methods brought up by artificial intelligence (AI) over the past half-century [SIM 73]. As future products cannot be deduced solely from existing knowledge, designers are here tasked with coercing (i.e. forcing) a futures creation process that is by design rational, repeatable, traceable, documentable, and transferable;

– supports the development of new breakthrough plans, solutions and alternatives with three novel and essential benefits: (i) help control the rationale of their developments; (ii) control and pace the degree of futures innovation (e.g. change, reform, progress, create, etc.) and the resulting time-scale futures lineages; (iii) support policy-makers in bringing the traced explanation of different design paths to decision.

*Representing dualistically (polarizing two spaces) and operating Arte (playing the C-K design square)*

> *"If the idea is not working with the hand, there is no artist."*

*"With Leonardo, everything seems to have two sides"* (Serge Bramly). An equal mixture of arts and sciences is a never failing postulate in Leonardo's works. His drawings bear a dual role: art (creation) and tools for scientific analysis (knowledge) while it remains just impossible to separate the two.

We could first associate scientific knowledge with the K space but practicing art isn't purely the C space as it needs a scientific understanding of the forms. Plus analyzing the forms of nature needs the artistic ability to draw them (akin to K). An intensive interlinking of features pertaining to art and science is rooting what we may confidently name innovating process.

Had a patent office operated during his days, he would have been eligible for thousands of patents, models, pictograms and copyrights, given his drawings and flanking notes joined in a pure play, a vivid and tutoring expression of ideas.

At first glance, his productions may seem to form a heterogeneous compilation: this isn't so. Instead they reveal an intense, deep and intricate whole; in a way, intelligence shows up at every pixel. While the notebooks contain cross-references between sparse drawings, deeper observation and analysis evidence the coherent and complex thinking process underpinning just all of his realizations. Actually, Leonardo's way is consistently built from three self-named constitutive elements:

– *scienzia*: meaning acquired, hopefully robust knowledge; which falls into the K-space;

– *fantasia*: or creative imagination; the C-space with the ability to expand in any conceivable way;

– *arte*: meaning skills, perhaps capacities; which we suggest to associate with the two reciprocal operators K➔C and C➔K of the design square. While a methodology for actuating the square is not clearly formalized in Da Vinci's Notebooks, lots of hints are available, which we will discuss.

"He insisted again and again that the art (skill) of painting must be supported by the painter's science (sound knowledge) of living forms" (Capra). This translates into: every single concept obtained from disjoining the K space is K-relative and the K space should never be left aside or lagging behind when progressing an overall design. The notebooks systematically juxtapose a drawing space and a textual notes space: he was capable of extracting knowledge given that he knew exactly where to make structure interact with content. A clear capacity to use knowledge models as a classification method.

As he was studying the science of art and reciprocally the art of science, he embarked in a creative, K-augmentation process. By leveraging this space, he professes a quest for knowledge robustness: "Ensure that you grasp the structure of all that you are endeavoring to paint. Each part is supposed to unite to the whole, which enables it to escape its own incompleteness."

By saying that (i) a painting is a whole that connects the parts – but the parts aren't left to themselves; therefore (ii) would they be so, they would tend to their "incompleteness" – i.e. the inherent blind spot or dead angle generated by the mere presence of the physical observation.

In other words, Da Vinci says that a mathematician's Continuum Hypothesis should be preserved in painting, incompleteness can be reached by a thinker, and that a painting should escape it. It took Gödel's famous 1931 intervention to prove the hypothesis false, then indirectly Cohen in 1963. Taine too praised his "*infinity greed, incapacity to be content*".

With *fantasia,* he generated ideas with a process that could impact creativity methods structurally:

1) Consult the information available anywhere (read: initiate a K0 mobilization) and induce a conceptual framework via a starting conceptual C0 point, e.g. a hypothesis or a blueprint.

2) Test ideas against own scientific observations, i.e. augment K and play C➔K operator.

3) Do not hesitate to modify older theories when experiments contradict them, i.e. reorder K.

A design process which evidences a tenacious use of C➔K and K➔C operators evokes Thomas Khun's definition of a scientific paradigm: *a constellation of concepts, value, perceptions, and practices.* As a result, art does not reside in the C space but in finding a constructive path toward the K space (although impressionism additionally emphasized the C space).

*Elaborating solid bodies of knowledge (or cognitive processes ever)*

> *"Mystery to Leonardo was a shadow, a smile and a finger pointing into darkness."*

Kenneth Clark

*In his direct observations of nature, Leonardo single-handedly developed a new approach to knowledge, known today as the scientific method.* No doubt the starting point is systematic observation, yet through the human eye and the brain; a concept that today we would state as cognition – the process of knowing. Leonardo wrote *"perspective is nothing else than a thorough knowledge of the function of the eye"* and much emphasized experience *(sperienza)* through methodical observation and experimentation. *"The painter is for Leonardo the cosmic eye which masters all visible things"* [WÖL 99].

Goethe insisted on his dominant eye-based talent that favored painting, who said *"he never accepted any arbitrary or fortuitous feature, everything had to be weighted up and thoughtful"*, and added: *"from pure proportion discovery to the most strange monsters made up with contradictory figures, all had to be natural and rational at the same time"*. Such a mixture evokes a C⯑K interplay that C-K theory carries on methodically. "All our knowledge has its origin in the senses; experience, mother of all certainty" are reflections of epochal naked eye observation limits, not so in "for he who can go to the well does not go to the water jar".

His anatomical drawings, which he calls *demostrazioni* ("demonstrations", or, would we say today, proofs of concepts or mock-ups), are typically not straight pictures of what one would see in an actual dissection but often bear an enhanced rendering (sometimes 3D-like). They are *"diagrammatic representations of the functional relationships between various parts of the body"* (Capra) that denote a superior – i.e. deep and intertwined knowledge.

Moreover, his scientific sketches are never representations of a single observation. Rather, they are syntheses of repeated studies, crafted in the form of theoretical models. *"Whenever Leonardo rendered objects in their sharp outlines, these pictures represented conceptual models rather than realistic images"* (Arasse). They are foundational elements in building scientific theories where the understanding of patterns, relationships and transformations becomes crucial for understanding the living world.

By writing "everything comes from everything, and everything is made of everything, and everything turns into everything, because that which exists in the elements is made up of these elements", Leonardo is creating K-complexity by way of a systemic – and not reductionist – way of thinking: not quantity first, but wholeness and quality. Which appears to be the way to understand knowledge in a multidisciplinary way – a *"knowledge bandwidth"*, in heavy demand today. Data doesn't have a bandwidth, being K base-band only; information may be contextual (have in-band K structure). But with Leonardo, information becomes action, i.e. knowledge-in-motion: mobilized and structured, a kosmos – an ordered and harmonious structure, ready to be organically exported to third receiving domains.

His resolutely systemic thought has bidirectional causal effects: "Mountains are built from rivers flows; mountains are destroyed by rivers flows", or "The earth is moved by the weight of a tiny bird who rests on it." *Facile cosa è farsi universale* said Leonardo of himself who "asked many questions nobody asked before and transcended the disciplinary boundaries of his time. He did so by *"recognizing patterns that interconnected forms and processes in different domains and by integrating his discoveries into a unified vision of the world"* (Capra). Though *"mutual generation of all parts of an organic whole"* (Capra; see Kant's self-organization), he creates, i.e. rhythms a wholeness.

### *Formulating root concepts (cognition – or plotting the undecidable)*

*"Material movement arises from the immaterial."*

*"Leonardo only knows the sole infinite, eternal space, in which his drawings likely seem to mesh. One proposes a sum of isolated and known objects within his paintings, the other a piece of the infinitum"* (Oswald Spengler). Leonardo would usually start from commonly accepted concepts and explanations, often summarizing before proceeding with his own observations, then formulating creative cognitive de-fixations. Example: a shadow "is" a cloth (or a variable

denoting absence of a luminous ray), "it clothes the bodies to which it is applied". He then jots down summaries in the form of many quick-sketched variations and even, after much investigation, as elaborate drawings.

His root concepts are often projected out of *fantasia* (K➔C) and retain distinct undecidable status at first. "The inventions of his *fantasia*, never out of harmony with universal dynamics as rationally comprehended, are fabulous yet not implausible, each element and their composition deriving from the causes and effects of the natural world" (Kemp). They amount to a "best start" which may perhaps reveal false later on, after complementary experiments (e.g. dissections, further observations…). A dual learning on how to form or vanish concepts: dying down concepts, subsuming them.

A story involving Steve Jobs and his original designer Jony Ive, comes to mind here.

*The story behind the creation of Sunflower iMac: Jobs, Ive and the sunflower in the garden*

One day, after his comeback to Apple, when a new Mac was about to be conceived, Steve and his first designer Jony Ive were walking in Jobs' garden at his home.

The first wasn't happy with what the second was proposing as a design for the new machine. Jobs walked with Ive in his garden:

> "As they walked through the 1,000-square-meter vegetable garden and apricot grove of Jobs' wife Laurene, Jobs sketched out the platonic ideal for the new machine. *Each element has to be true to itself,* Jobs told Ive. *Why have a flat display if you're going to glom all this stuff on its back? Why stand a computer on its side when it really wants to be horizontal and on the ground? Let each element be what it is, be true to itself.* Instead of looking like the old iMac, the thing should look more like the flowers in the garden. Jobs said, *It should look like a sunflower.*"

Biodesign that is directly inspired from nature. That model sparked the iMac Sunflower, which succeeded the egg-shaped 1998 iMac G3.

The extract is from Time Magazine: http://www.time.com/time/magazine/article/0,9171,192601,00.html.

As he makes progress in his understanding of natural phenomena in one area, he becomes aware of the interconnecting patterns to phenomena in other areas and revises his putative ideas accordingly. Leonardo called all human creations "artifacts", and works of art "inventions" (Capra referred to him as *inventor and interpreter between nature and humans*, i.e. who created an artifact or work of art by assembling various elements into a new configuration that didn't appear in nature). This specification comes ever closer to our definition of a designer. Leonardo's *disegnatore* term always means draftsman and he also uses *compositore*.

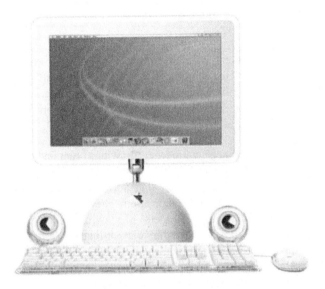

**Figure A3.2.** *The "sunflower" made artifact or inspiration right from the garden. This iMac G4 relaunched Apple as a genuinely first rate innovator in 2002 (source: http://theoryofnames.com/wp-content/uploads/2012/10/sunflower-image-2.jpg - Sunflower iMac aka iMac G4)*

A striking formulation of root concepts comes through the interplay of opposites (or making conceptual expansion). Leonardo embodied a dynamic tension between contradictory paradoxes in his personality. He was also fascinated by opposites through his life. By consistently practicing conceptual separation, he extracted separate mechanisms (gears, levers, bearings, couplings, etc.) from the machines in which they were embedded. Examples of such root concepts with expansive property: a table lamp with "variable" intensity; doors that open and close "automatically" (by means of counterweights); {folding} furniture; how a human pilot might "generate enough force" to lift a flying machine off the ground (by flapping its mechanical wings); an octagonal mirror that "generates an infinite number of multiple images", a spit in which the roast will turn "slow or fast" depending whether the fire is moderate or strong. These codes expansively splinter as many dominant designs.

## A3.4. On the value of the analysis

*On the process of emergence of design process (or embodying resulting concepts)*

> *"Knowing is not enough; we must apply. Being willing is not enough; we must do."*

A process of embodiment is an invitation to experiment. In Leonardo's works, it's both a unifying cognitive representation of a seamless art/science unity and a tool that he uses for scientific analysis or forms understanding. His drawings aim to assert that they give "true knowledge of shapes, which is impossible without an immense, tedious and confused amount of writing and time".

By contrast, Renaissance engineers' drawings remain explanatory, while Leonardo's are engaging, convincing, even compelling, persuading the viewer of the feasibility and design soundness by inviting a viewer's questioning at knowledge level through aesthetic visual contextualization. They bear the concrete appearance of objects that exist. Examples: the angle(s) of view, the subtlety of shadows, their background treatment "all give them an extraordinary persuasive effectiveness" (Arasse). Furthermore, many drawings mix "the coldness of the scientific investigations with the emotional emphasis" (Nathan). Meaning, motion, engagement…speak for the emergence of a design science.

In preparatory drawings, he would go over a figure again and again, sketching several alternative lines and variations of position, until the ideal form be found. He tries out different possibilities: what are the different ways to represent the problem?

These sketches have high dynamic quality, a brainstorm of dynamic sketching. "Never before had any artist worked out his compositions in such a welter of alternative lines" (Kemp). "Such flexibility of preparatory sketching became the norm for later centuries; it was introduced almost single-handedly by Leonardo" (Capra). In movement, his eye perceives the hidden, latent, buried form striving to become a figure. First I shall do some experiments before I proceed further, because my intention is to cite experience first and then with reasoning show why such experience is bound to operate in such a way.

*"And this is the true rule by which those who speculate about the effects of nature must proceed"* (Leonardo in 1513). Concepts are thus drawn in C first, then grow as K representatives, ready for varied take ups.

## Assessing designs and field explorations (or assessment criteria)

*"Art is never finished, only abandoned."*

What would be the perfect value criteria for Leonardo? That *"an ingenuous design be created, beautiful, easy and economical, in which nothing is wanting and nothing is superfluous"* (he's describing nature). He sees as useful to distinguish deep values (transposable, value for another domain: cross-innovation impact, verifiability: robustness) from shallow values (conceptual clarity, richness of alternatives, discovery of a transcending "invention": originality, multidisciplinary spread: variety). Yet, how does Leonardo structure, compare, and assess design paths more specifically?

1) *Originality.* *"The solutions he imagines are invariably unconventional"* (Arasse). Examples: simultaneously gothic and Mannerist, effortless integration of architecture and complex geometry, many designs of centralized, radially symmetric churches and "temples". *"Design for centralized temple is reminiscent of fractals: a mathematical integration of the parts, a sense of organic unity, the spatial vision which allows him to display his design as a fully 3D concept"* (Capra). His cognitive depth and, as said above, expansive partitioning in C, serve an unconventional renewal of concepts.

2) *Variety.* "The parameters of the experimental setting are varied in order to bring to light the essential unchanging features of the phenomena being investigated. He would often vary his parameters systematically to test the consistency of the results" (Capra). In conducting experiments, Da Vinci stresses the need for careful repetitions and variations. Painting Madonna and Child with Saint Anne took more than a decade (not an isolated example by far!), during which he made numerous drawings with variations on compositional and theological themes. He often uses catalogs of geometrical representations for de-fixing concepts (e.g. the concept of mapping as: transforming a circle into an ellipse; a gradual movement; a flow under continuous change), or uses motion with a sense of relationship to actual or potential forms where he will find transitional examples.

3) *Variable expansion.* His notebooks contain examples of experiments he conducted again and again by just changing one variable. An arresting example is the bewildering 2-folios study of the activity of the lunulas of Hippocrates of Chios (only mathematically proven recently). Comparison (paragone) *He used blue wash of varying hues to produce a striking resemblance between the flow of the river's watercourses and the flow of blood in the bodies' veins.* Comparing the dome of a church to the human cranium, or vaulting arches and rib cage, or body metabolism process (ebb and flow of respiration, blood transport of nutrients) with a building

"metabolism" (how stairs and doors facilitate movement through it), or a human blood vessels diagram next to sketches of stairs, or water as the veins of a living Earth. Genericizing by juxtaposition. The above contextual conversions amount to a code for obtaining a generic property by overlaying domains. Not seeking solutions, but domains!

4) *Robustness and integration.* "*For Leonardo, painting is an operation requiring all the available knowledge and almost all the known techniques – geometry, dynamics, geology, physiology. A battle to show up supposes whirls and lifted dust; and yet, he wants only to represent them after having observed them with eyes waiting to become learned and as if wholly penetrated by the knowledge of their laws*" (Valéry). Complex secondary effects of light-reflected sheens, areas of diffused light, subtle glows. The garden is an integral part of the house. Milan after the plague: he sees the city as a kind of living organism. The Sala delle Asse: contents interlink with each other to form a harmonious whole. Descartes compared science to a tree (*"the roots are metaphysics, the trunk is physics, the branches are all other sciences"*); in anticipatory contrast, Leonardo's science is already a complex interconnectedness of the branches of many trees! His unified vision of the world is highly relevant to our times (patterns of relationships, i.e. systemic knowledge) and places blazing calls for a universal science, while his exploration codes enhance reliability and functionality performance.

Let's note that his architectural drawings are not imprecise: they're free of details! It is the logical linking and the reciprocal organization of the part of, for example, the building, that interests him. In other words, the problems addressed are theoretical problems of architectural design and the questions he asks are the same which he explores throughout his science of organic forms: patterns, spatial organization, rhythm, flow.

EXAMPLES.– Living and non-living forms (studying the flight patterns of birds to create flying machines); anatomy: workings of the human heart, circulatory system; turbulence of water: vast knowledge of hydraulics, rebuilding Milan's infrastructure, the plain of Lombardy (city planners still use these principles); growth patterns: of grasses; military: weights and levers, trajectories and forces, weapons and defenses (fortifications), optics, nature of light, etc.

In summary, Leonardo exceeds traditional criteria assessing an innovation and scores the maximum over the innovation capability maturity model scale [COR 15].

## Unceasingly mapping cross disciplinary (or ever in search for conjunctions)

> "*A poet knows he has achieved perfection not when there is nothing left to add, but when there is nothing left to take away.*"

Leonardo never sees an own explanation as final (early view: *the heart is a stove housing a central fire*; later view: *the heart is a muscle pumping blood through the arteries*) but considers semantic networks.

EXAMPLES.– Water at the center: a medium of life; a source of power: trade systems; air and wind flows: investigated through birds flights, flying machines, aerodynamic principles; etc.

In a distinctive operating way, Leonardo works on many problems simultaneously. This enables him to pay special attention to similarities of forms and processes in different areas of investigation, including natural phenomena: living forms in different species exhibit patterns similarities. By understanding the processes and the forces underlying the formation, he compares organic forms and processes, studies homologies (structural correspondences between different species) due to their evolutionary descent from a common ancestor (inspired from Capra, as well as the below lists).

*Comparisons of forms/patterns*

The forces transmitted by pulleys and levers and transmitted by muscles, tendons and bones; mechanics: the tensions in cords, levers and pulleys as in tendons and muscles; patterns of turbulence in water and in air; the flow of water and of human hair; the leg of a man and of a horse; reflection of light on a surface and mechanical rebound of a ball thrown against a wall, and the echo of the sound and the jet of water from a wall (*"The voice is similar to an object seen in a mirror"*); spiraling whirlpools and coiling foliage of certain plants; the veins in the human body behave like oranges, *in which, as the skin thickens, so the pulp diminishes the older they become*; in The Battle of Anghiari painting, comparing expressions of fury in the faces of a man and a horse, and a lion; the flow of sap in a plant or tree and in the human body – the vital sap of plants as their essential life fluid, nourishes the plant's tissues as blood nourishes the human body; the structural similarity between the stalk (funiculus) and the umbilical cord attaching the human fetus to the placenta (unity of life at all scales of nature); the circular light pattern with the circular spread of ripples of water, with the spread of sound in air; etc.

*Interconnecting K domains*

To Da Vinci, understanding human form means understanding the body in motion, which is often reflected by an emphasis on proportions: proportions of human body $\Leftrightarrow$ of buildings; interlinking animal physiology and engineering to understand the animal body movements $\Leftrightarrow$ exploring principles of mechanics; investigations of muscles/bones $\Leftrightarrow$ studies and drawings of gears/levers; patterns of turbulence in water $\Leftrightarrow$ in air flows; science of living forms $\Leftrightarrow$ of movement and transformation; nature of sound ⇔ music theory, design of musical instruments; inspiration from science of transformations in mountains, rivers, plants ⇔ in human body; motion transformed into rhythm (the painting of the Last Supper conveys gestures emotions and sentiments); etc.

### Counter analogies

"*The spiral or rotary movement of a liquid is so much swifter as it is nearer to the center of its revolution but the circular movement of the wheel is so much slower as it is nearer to the center of the rotating object*", an observation that had to wait 350 years for Helmholtz. Opposing views, water as "diluting matter": "*without water nothing retains its natural form*" *(dynamic stability).*

### Metaphors

The flow of water represented through a channel of various cross-sections by using a model of rows of men marching through a street of varying width. When studying water: "*take knowledge of the movement of a water surface, that behaves like hair, which has two directions, one that follows its own weight, and the other the loops injunctions; same wise, water describes swirling curves, of which one part follows the main current flow and the other the fortuitous and induced movement.*" (Zöllner).

## A3.5. Wrapping up the key elements of relevance to Apple

*Theory infused in "sperienza" (or an enduring Leonardo/C-K thread)*

> "*Simplicity is the ultimate sophistication.*"

Practicing Da Vinci-based methodological lines exposed C-K theory in five extensive ways:

– exercising the design square. C-K theory design power parallels Leonardo's approaches to using the environment. All four operators are put into use through *Scientia, Fantasia and Arte*;

– elaborating deep cognitive processes, with an intense propensity to force knowledge mobilization, by e.g. compositing sparse observations, plus constantly reordering knowledge;

– playing with many variation techniques, e.g. opposites, with surprising de-fixing effect;

– valuing everything in direct connection with augmenting knowledge base relentlessly;

– the (almost massively) concurrent designing and engineering approach that he favored so ardently hided, and now reveal, a quest for genericity that is only matched by most recent industrial design research. Leonardo does much more with much less because he finds what's underpinning. We would say he captures the DNA of things, by somewhat grasping the fabric of nature.

While "his focus was the nature of organic form" (Capra), Leonardo Da Vinci's approach to art and science offers an experiential key to C-K theory and contributes to validating it experimentally. Even more, it seemingly pioneered several ideas encapsulated in it. Being Leonardo a genuine template of a transdisciplinary genius, whose worldview was not mechanistic but organic and ecological, his legacy may even instruct and guide the C-K practitioner in at least two ways:

– *disciplinary defragmentation.* By not separating epistemology (the theory of knowledge) from ontology (the theory of what exists in the world), or philosophy from science and art, he freed cross-domains innovation processes. Examples: from perspective to effects of light and shade, to the nature of light, to the pathways of optic nerves, the "actions of the soul";

– *bringing forward complexity views.* Leonardo invariably emphasized the wholeness of things and *fundamental interdependence of all natural phenomena,* and the unity of things – a most humanistic view. C-K theory comes as a systemic conception of the process of knowing and its language blends several languages, in particular all those of a design activity. By widening C-K formulations at systemic level, defragmenting their disciplinary understandings, and disentangling reductionist frameworks, C-K theory tends to build a network of inseparable patterns of relationships which bear the power to redress, through design innovation, some of the complex economic, environmental and technological problems.

Such blended skill set is commanding. He seems too to expand C-K theory along two directions:

1) An engaging feature is his genuine ability to operate systemically, a trait humanity is still presently learning the hard way. *With the rise of systemic thinking and its emphasis on networks, complexity, and patterns of organization, we can now more fully appreciate the power of Leonardo's science and its relevance for our [post-]modern era.* Rather than focusing on the countless overwhelming results, he admirably achieved in many different fields. By engaging in *discorso mentale*

(mental discourse), the intellectual process of painting today becomes competitively more valuable than the actual completion of the work.

2) Through the "unifying picture of natural phenomena", which Capra denoted, he's able to open up a remarkable strategy for genericity in designing objects in that he: (i) indifferently works at several or many projects concurrently; (ii) directly addresses a bundle of different situations and problems, as if he had a capitalization platform at hand supposedly capable of providing him with answers, even if not solutions yet, which yields a genuine scaling up faculty. While routinely taking up multitudes of projects at once, he looks for common descriptors and properties and detaches them from their initial observed environment. Then, develops a "generic kernel" by superposition, away from specific constraints and which properties he applies widely (yet, he doesn't explicit context-independent generic assertions). All is reminiscent of recent work by Kokshagina [KOK 13] in using design theory for designing generic technology and founding a theory of genericity in design.

## A basket of paradoxes? (or you need ecosystems)

> "I have offended God and mankind because my work didn't reach the quality it should have."

Many original facets of Leonardo's work have been neglected so far, his work having had an utmost emphasis of interest on the outcomes and not on the method, if any. Filling this gap unearths singular implications for education and management as society still resorts to sequential planning in execution situations and linear thinking in teaching: we have yet to tackle complexity upfront. Leonardo did, and thus benefited from a scaling up ability. Should Leonardo be a post-modern design innovation consultant, he would presumably work not in, but across all domains and industrial sectors concurrently, interconnect them, being gifted in each single project with an extreme compartmentalization for achieving every single piece of art or engineering, etc., while still mastering perfection.

Recent literature [SCH 15] dissects another, more recent exemplar: "*Steve [Jobs] was capable of extraordinary compartmentalization*" while "*helping him turn around Apple*". Leonardo capitalizes on mixed situations in depth, thus minimizing the space between design activity and his "real world", instead of doing separate projects: how long would it take to perform his works one at a time? This suggests that design is an intrinsically global activity.

Huge masses of books depicting Da Vinci's realizations have hypnotized us with his plentiful, often unbelievable achievements, yet, besides Fritjof Capra to some extent, their vast majority fell short of digging a Master's way: his thinking and operating codes before the yields (a key to advancing design thinking may be understanding processes). This appendix evidenced the following relative key elements:

– Leonardo's operation codes are strategies for enhancing a man's knowledge, yet, he fell short of widely sharing his intellectual capital (which was his regular income) except for his contracted work with clients and factions. He "*did not share his scientific knowledge although he shared his knowledge of painting with fellow artists and disciples*" (Capra). He had "*no real understanding of the way in which the growth of knowledge was a collaborative process*" (Hope). His still enduring legacy indicates that Leonardo (not a mere thinker but an utmost doer) exemplifies a unique operating model: working alone with rare helpers, yet talking "straight to mankind".

– In this avatar-like position, the Da Vinci-to-mankind model delivers a "genius ecosystem" capacity that can map out much of engineering design thinking. What if we applied his way collectively and collaboratively? What if clusters of organizations – becoming "Living Ecosystems" beyond Living Labs – would operate Leonardo ways? Partners attracting systems and vice versa in an accelerated whirl of coherent innovation capacity.

All this amounts to elevating design innovation to the rank of a fully-fledged liberal art. C-K Theory is a collective and cooperative dance in which creativity and constant re-commissioning of knowledge are driving forces. That such a theory comes of age about five centuries after an ancestral Da Vinci's method may be seen as a confident sign, as depicted in this annex, of mankind ability to methodically progress from singular science, creativity, and arts achievements. C-K theory may appear apt to making up the "Leonardo way" of our post-modern times, prefiguring steady avalanches of interwoven innovations for mankind.

Still, with the recent emphasis on complexity, networks, and patterns of organization, could a new science of quality be emerging? Wouldn't a more thorough investigation of a handful of most remarkable selected personalities, artists and engineers alike, be poised to offer a basis for undertaking a real paradigmatic change in our education and management methods for future generations – a new intelligence tooling for society?

And, after five hundred years of relative factual analysis concerning Da Vinci works, would it be a too distant goal to set for the advancement of mankind? Hippolyte Taine would likely not object, he who praised his extreme forward-thinking inclination "*beyond his century and the following ones*". Same for Steve Jobs, who is likely to inspire both business leaders and business schools for the decades to come?

## Acknowledgments

Thanks to Dr. Philippe Blanchard – an Apple Distinguished Educator – from École du Bois, Nantes, France, for bringing a number of textual formatting improvement to the contents of this appendix.

# Appendix 4

## Further Tips in Designing Innovations with C-K Theory

*"How can I go forward when I don't know which way I'm facing."*

John Lennon

These transformation elements are drained from C-K theory and other research and help in transforming the genes into actionable patterns of innovation. The practice of identifying, defining, and then breaking dominant designs roots the art of breakthrough innovation in industry and elsewhere, including in arts and civil crafts.

### A4.1. Tracking dominant designs above all

Marketed objects[1] are bound to a structuring reference for organizing trade: the design is shared by players, including competitors; markets are rather mature[2]: "The value of objects can be assessed, products are endorsed by competitors, knowledge can be accumulated, and all changes followed on. One virtue of a dominant design is to simplify the offer-demand relationship. Incremental innovation may be performed to sustain a dominant design. In the end, dominant designs evolve to the point of sheer complexity, hence may call for self alteration; then, new dynamics emerge that break dominant designs down".

---

1 The word "object" will be understood in a general way: a product, service, actually anything that can be subject to innovating, i.e. altering its "identity".
2 From the podcast *First steps in fielding C-K theory*, by P. Blanchard and P. Corsi (2013), available at the Apple Store.

The notion of dominant design traces back to Utterback and Abernathy [UTT 75, ABE 78, UTT 94].

## A4.2. Why they (still) exist

Industry typically operates by favoring a relatively stable categorization of products, market segments, players, etc. and even ecosystems. This has evident advantages: competition can be set, organized and strive.

By doing so, its means of action are making key market assumptions:

– objects' identities are as stable as possible: functionality and performance can be referred to;

– delegation can be organized (supply chains, research, development...) and specialized departments become in charge of a key dimension of the work;

– then, planning is based on linear models, which are bound to predictive and other statistical analysis approaches;

– and, finally, the classical management models with respect to objectives can operate, also by using the many well-known methods, techniques and tools such as market and value analysis, portfolio management, change management, business process re-engineering, etc.

## A4.3. Why they still work (less and less)

However, can the above be a safe harbor for long? Are products really permanent? It is the quintessential function of innovation to alter a status quo. For sure, innovation can create a roller coaster game both for clients (who then have to re-learn about products and usages) and competitors (who can't rest assured on agreed market grounds safely shared by all). Innovation is that spoofy catalyst that, when regulated with care, transforms entire industry domains with no possible return, ever.

As soon as innovation forces drive the competition, the above assumptions and model of industrial activity gradually lose their validity:

– object identities are altered continuously, without an *a priori* commonly agreed plan, stifling the stable references industry was building from;

– specialized departments need to intertwine their operations deeper and deeper, for example, R&D can no longer be distinct from marketing;

– statistics become insufficient to feed the plans and methods, which shift from reactive to proactive, even anticipative;

– and, finally, the organization can no longer be managed "incrementally" based on identified resources, bound to fixed objectives, and on fixed division of labor.

When innovation becomes intensively called forth, the traditional settings of industry not only lose their value but represent, as time goes on, an impediment to become dynamically agile, and to regenerate itself at times. If flexibility shall rule, it would be at the expenses of rigidities everywhere: structural (hierarchies and commandment), organizational (competences, procedures, etc.) and operational (from R&D to markets and back).

## A4.4. What would an industry breaker do?

The method is simple to explain:

1) *Accept the industry's dominant designs (DD) and understand where they come from.*

You can't fool them but, by understanding where they originate from, you gain a key to an exit door. For instance, by realizing "banking is important, banks are not" (a famous quote from Bill Gates), you wouldn't position banks at the center of a business ecosystem when dealing with billing procedures. Instead, you would attempt to understand why banks were created and for which original functions. focusing on the transaction act itself and secure the passage only, by getting rid of all other dimensions, actually becoming de facto contingencies. And this is potentially revolutionary.

2) *Locate a few of them and dig out their functioning.*

You're not at the exit door yet, venturing in an unknown land. You need to first scope each DDs found well: do I need it? Is it optional? Who controls it? Do alternatives exist? So you prune them and extract a short list upon which to forward your new venture. The rest of the basket of DDs goes to the back burner for the time being for later steering.

This step presupposes a lot of leaning ability from the part of the company.

3) *Find a point of break and open it.*

Breaking a dominant design is the door to venturing into the unknown. By removing the locks that express anterior compromised methods and solutions, entire avenues of new possibilities can see the light of day, as long as the new choices are sound, a thing no market analysis can prove to you nor prove it remains impossible. The postulated choices are but undecidable at this stage. Those who dare to venture through may be rewarded with surprisingly successful bets. The trick will be to express the dominant designs in a way that they can be broken for exploring what it would mean then for the product. After which step, rupture axes need to be defined and explored.

The following illustrates what Apple has performed in terms of breaking the locks.

4) *Later, intentionally create dominant designs regimes.*

Here enter the notion of lineage ("a matching of key competencies and product families" [LEM 10]) whereby:

– new knowledge has been created;

– a products lineage is created by reusing this knowledge;

– hybridization follows that aims at exploring all possible strategic market spaces corresponding to that new knowledge.

Through a succession of products, a stabilization path can thus be forged where innovation is still present. Dosed variations in product functionality, design, performance, etc., make the road to sustained presence on markets.

Because the client has to go through new learning processes each time a lineage is created, the new knowledge put on the market should be as intuitive as feasible. Then, the lineage process itself creates a virtuous "endogenous customer learning process" [LEM 10] that, for instance, Apple has been mastering epochally: a Mac user shall learn it all just by doing.

Reciprocally, the firm learns from customer experience throughout the entire lineage process.

## A4.5. Conclusion

We are far from offer and demand, market saturation first principles and market erosion phenomena. When lineages prevail, the firm cannot preserve its past hierarchies and organizational methods but becomes more and more a "swarm" organization, dwelling into complexities at every stage of its operations.

As dominant designs in lineages follow classical S-shaped curves (slow growth first, then high growth, followed by slow growth at high output [LEM 10]), the industry regenerates a traditional pattern of mature industries anchored on their dominant designs. Those companies having a "revolutionary" DNA cannot content with this fate and will compulsively prefer to enter a radically new game, by again, breaking yet another dominant design. And here, we ever see Apple at its best. A compulsory evolutionary destiny of a born-catalyst.

# Appendix 5

## Tips on Deepening Understanding by Using Trialectics

*"Uniting without confusing and distinguishing without separating."*

The trialectics motto

### A5.1. Introducing trialectics

This appendix introduces a ternary methodology of thought processes, named "trialectics", as a tool for deepening the multidimensional understanding of any concept. It was conceived by Gérard Gigand [GIG 15] over several years and is used in various environments ranging from executive coaching to professional consulting. Trialectics is useful to deepen the understanding of the innovation intensity at Apple.

We position trialectics as a genuine methodology (method of methods) with two essential properties:

1) It proposes a systematic ternary thinking approach to perform conceptual variations and expansions relatively to three fundamental and generic invariants: incompleteness, auto-reference and indeterminacy.

2) It helps formulating systemic concepts that clarify the expression of the initial concept.

Trialectics supports the development of C-K diagrams further, especially enhancing originality and variety when exploring the concepts in the C space. For doing so, we target the two terms, "competitiveness" and "innovativeness", whose diagrams are elaborated in Chapters 17 and 18, for approaching specific features pertaining to Apple's capacity under these two keystone fields of operations. Ours is a unique approach to know what can be understood in a motto such as "think different" in deeper ways.

Trialectics has profound roots in the complexity of phenomena, a fundamental thinking that began in the 1960s and for which Edgar Morin [MOR 04] has been an outstanding forerunner. It posits the existence of the limit in the face of the knowable: how to know in the face of infinitum? How can thought thinks of itself?

Here, knowledge and actions are connected; this relational approach to knowledge leads to transdisciplinarity. A binary approach is based on antagonisms and "excluded thirds". Trialectics, a genuine ternary approach, produces "smoother antagonisms" differentiated at various degrees. The resulting gradation in antagonistic relationship is capable to harness the systemic interactions present in contextualizing concepts.

The approach is instrumental in:

– uniting and merging concepts without confounding them;

– distinguishing among concepts without severing them.

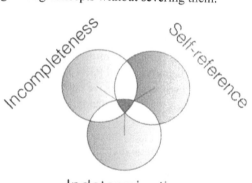

Indetermination

**Figure A5.1.** *The three fundamental invariants at work. At the very center, the property of unknowability rules*

## A5.2. Using trialectics

The use of trialectics, a method based on complexity, requires thinking of the relations between concepts. Five operators are used in sequence: invariants, attractors, influence agents, non-symmetrical antagonisms and including thirds.

What results captures the essence of the initial concept through a relational cartography of words. The resulting words are concepts that will be fed in C-K diagrams.

Let's discuss the three invariants first:

– *Incompleteness*. It is the blind spot, the dead angle generated by the presence of our physical observation: *"where I see from, I can't see"*. It induces a partial knowledge (in deficit) of the object of perception. It also concerns a "critical mass" beyond which the object destroys itself. However, it does not mean "unfinished".

– *Self-reference*. It is self-persuasion, self-appropriation or involvement: *"within the field allowing my perception, I can see what I want to see"*. Our perception is the outcome of a personal interpretation implying a partial knowledge (biased) of the object of perception – a viewpoint. For instance, the conscious process of observing innovation integrates an auto-referring dimension which we perceive as "deviance from the mainstream". However, self-reference does not mean self-centeredness.

– *Indeterminacy*. It underpins a choice, or is background flexibility, or focusing: *"within the field allowing my perception, the precision of my vision requires a selection"*. Hence, another form of partial knowledge (selectivity, resolution and fragmentation). However, it does not mean vagueness.

The three forms "knowledge partiality" constitute the generic triple limit of the process of perception. It is essential to distinguish between the three statuses:

*Unknown – Uncertain – Indeterminated*

We can link each of them to three fundamental pillars in science and philosophy:

– *Incompleteness links to Gödel's 1931 theorems*. They say in essence that any logics formalism that includes arithmetics also contains undecidable assertions: that are not demonstrable by applying the formalism rules.

– *Self-reference links to Kant and Heisenberg*. In essence, no observation is objective. Reality can be accessed, but not designed as an object per se, only through self-referencing, subject and object together.

– *Indeterminacy links to Heisenberg's fundamental work*. Our perception requests accuracy and therefore will strive to select and focus. Perception engages a degree of resolution which is constrained by how we observe. Any precision is selective. Understanding the observation entails a selection, a scoping and a focusing. Paradoxically, it is indeterminacy that permits rigor and Werner Heisenberg is of great help in this matter.

## A5.3. Operating trialectics on the concept of "Brand"

Given an initial concept to work on, trialectics operates the five operators (invariants, attractors, influence agents, non-symmetrical antagonisms and including thirds) in four main phases:

1) Identifying the three-dimensional *attractors*. They are "the influence of the three invariants on the root theme". They delimit the validity domain of the initial concept. The dimensions are respective to the three invariants (incompleteness, self-reference, indeterminacy).

2) Defining the *influencing agents* (6) and the *antagonisms* (6).

3) Defining the resulting three "*including thirds*".

4) Synthesizing the findings. The resulting analysis uniquely deepens the understanding of the initial concept.

The trialectics process engages a relational analysis throughout because it invites the thinking on a relational and dynamic understanding of the concept at hand:

– what are the various dimensions of the concept or the phenomena studied?

– what are the interwoven aspects, given the radical unknowability underpinning any observation that is conscious of its own limits?

Let us operate the method on a relevant example, *branding*. In Chapter 4, we match the present findings with the Apple brand. The working out of a trialectics diagram is not easy at first glance and routinely requires a collective effort. But, the value that results is worth the effort as it lightens the initial concept by unparalleled understanding.

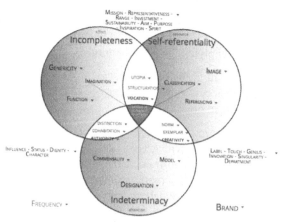

**Figure A5.2.** *Working through the notion of brand with the trialectics methodology: a first diagram captures the intrinsic dimensional powers of a brand*

Figure A5.2 evidences the dimensional image/genericity/designation trilogy for any brand and ends up with the three "including thirds": *vocation, creativity* and *authority*. This chart lays out where the power of correct branding resides.

Let us first define the three attractors based on the three generic invariants:

– The incompleteness of a brand is ultimately the notion of *genericity*: where it looses its peculiar specificity. A generic product is the limit of a specific product.

– The self-referentiality of a brand is simply the *image* it produces on our perception.

– The indeterminacy of a brand is its relative capacity to *designate* a particular category of product.

Having obtained the three attractors, we now derive six agents (three pairs):

– The influence of the incompleteness attractor on image is only bounded by *imagination*. Reciprocally, the influence of self-referentiality onto genericity is the unavoidable *classification* that results.

– The influence of incompleteness on designation reduces to the *function* itself. Reciprocally, the influence of indeterminacy on genericity is the communalized degree, or *commensality* (an old word signifying the sharing capacity at a same *mensa* or host table).

– The influence of self-referentiality on designation is the referencing that results, or *referentiation*. Reciprocally, the influence of indeterminacy on image is the relative *model* that may be used.

Having now the six agents, working the method ends ends by contrasting these two-by-two. We reduce the three antagonisms obtained as follows:

– Imagination and classification come together (fuse and integrate) into *utopia,* and contrast into *structuration*. Then, we resolve these into the "including third", named *vocation*.

– Function and commensality unite into *cohabitation*, and maximize their disparity into *distinction*. We resolve the two views into *authority*.

– Referentiation and model blend into *norm*, and diverge into *exemplar*. We resolve the two perspectives with the word *creativity*.

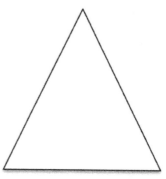

VOCATION
(mission, scope, representativity, finality…)

AUTHORITY
(statute, dignity, character…)

CREATIVITY
(genius, mark, innovation…)

**Figure A5.3.** *The resulting three so-called "including thirds" are essential synthetic representatives of the initial notion (here, the "brand")*

At this stage, what remains to perform is an interpretive explanation of the findings. In the present case of a brand, we begin to sense the peculiar pulsation that it is supposed to exert in its environment. There is a notion of persistence and beat, both density and exactness, or fidelity in a genuine brand, which explains why the word *frequency* can be suggested as a definite and definitive whole compositing the building aspects of the concept of brand.

In the case of Apple, the exposition of the intermediary words and the synthetic essence is provided in Chapter 4. The findings denote a particularly appreciative and robust brand.

A second chart (Figure A5.4) focuses on the routine use of a brand, its category, exposure and appropriate authentication aspects. A mundane object that pervades our lives, showing *meaning* (is it addiction or a generic affair?), *recognition* (identifying it in sociable settings) and a degree of *confusion* (what degree of (in-) significance, perhaps imitated?).

The reason we show these two diagrams is to unequivocally show how definite, strict and specific the Apple brand has become through the years: a scrupulously distinct symbol resonating with the first diagram. The Apple frequency is a clear-cut emblem.

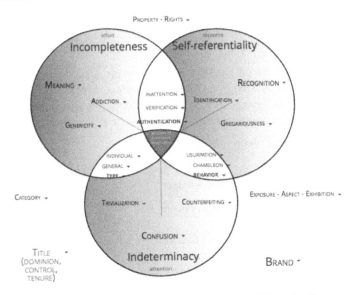

**Figure A5.4.** *Working through the notion of brand with the trialectics methodology: a second diagram enhances the more mundane values of a brand*

## A5.4. Articulating trialectics with C-K theory

C-K theory introduces the systemic interplay between concepts and knowledge. By concepts we mean propositions that are neither true nor false, that you cannot prove anything about, just conjecture. Our mind experiences difficulty in accepting that something seems a sort of negation of knowledge, a non-knowledge. Zen masters instruct that the key to radical evolution lies in the art of transcending contradictions. In Western culture, oxymorons are well known (e.g. a bitter sweet sauce, a virtual reality, a working holiday, a peace force, a dark light, etc.). Oxymoronic expressions actually open a fantasy space that contains nothing.

Such emptiness can spark a whole creation cycle. Accepting to start from an empty space is an act of transcending humility found in great innovators and artists of all vests: it calls for dipping in infinite realms. Formally, the implication:

{contradictions, oxymorons, etc.}→∅(empty starting space for designing new concepts)

But, how would you sanely start from an empty space? Frank Zappa had his eclectic quote: "*Art is making something out of nothing and selling it*". Hatchuel and Weil [HAT 07] found the way thanks to post-modern mathematics. Trialectics gives insights for working with any concept C at three specific stages:

1) when disjoining C from reference knowledge K;

2) when expanding C systematically through the addition (or suppression) of attributes that are dependent on knowledge;

3) when joining back a resulting concept X to the knowledge space.

When starting with trialectics, the three attractors open an initial expansion which already ontologically maximizes the power of the variety criterion. This is of interest for practitioners, as they genuinely strive to place the high-level conceptual expansions as close as possible to the root concept at hand. Increasing expansion power goes by using either the antagonisms created between the six agents or the including thirds which result from them.

## A5.5. Conclusion

Using C-K theory specifies a design practice in particular. The trialectics approach evidences that the border between the "singularities" in knowledge and its practice is not clear because they are present in each other. Further, it makes the clarification of their coextensive relation and singular identity a subject of study "par excellence". We found that such study deepens conceptual disjunctions, expansions and conjunctions when operating in the context of implementing C-K theory. The virtue of trialectics is to be found in refining two of the four value criteria of C-K theory, those more concerned with the conceptual C space, and in these terms:

– *Variety*. Distinguishing without severing. Trialectics diagrams unfold progressively. The interrelatedness of the successive agents (renamed agents and including thirds) ensure they don't separate.

– *Originality*. Combining without merging. Single trialectics diagrams combine as one whole (any is co-extensive of the others). They don't merge as the three invariant dimensions bear singular authority.

Together with C-K theory, the application of trialectics to mundane target problematics at first reinforces and redefines the rapport between knowledge and practice. Moreover, it also helps a decisive diving into the unknown due to its unique methodology rooted on the pioneering works of Gödel, Kant and Heisenberg.

# Appendix 6

## Selected Quotes from Steve Jobs

The following quotes from the late Steve Jobs have been selected on the basis of their relevance to the genes list. Many more could retain similar interest for the purpose of this book. However, the authors encourage referring to the many appropriate Websites as well as to the reference bibliography.

*"I wish developing great products was as easy as writing a check. If that was the case, Microsoft would have great products."*

*CNET*, May 10, 2007.

*"We did iTunes because we all love music. We made what we thought was the best jukebox in iTunes. Then we all wanted to carry our whole music libraries around with us. The team worked really hard. And the reason that they worked so hard is because we all wanted one. You know? I mean, the first few hundred customers were us."*

*Fortune*, March, 2008.

*"The people who built Silicon Valley were engineers. They learned business, they learned a lot of different things, but they had a real belief that humans, if they worked hard with other creative, smart people, could solve most of humankind's problems. I believe that very much."*

*Wired*, Feb. 1996

*"Companies, as they grow to become multibillion-dollar entities, somehow lose their vision. They insert lots of layers of middle management between the people running the company and the people doing the work. They no longer have an inherent feel or a passion about the products. The creative people, who are the ones who care passionately, have to persuade five layers of management to do what they know is the right thing to do."*

*Playboy*, Feb., 1985

*"Software is what will distinguish products in the next 10 years. And I think the technology for software is just starting to come into its own."*

*Newsweek*, Sept. 29, 1985

*"It's in Apple's DNA that technology alone is not enough – it's technology married with liberal arts, married with the humanities, that yields us the result that makes our heart sing, and nowhere is that more true than in these post-PC devices."*

*Seattle Times*, March 3, 2011.

*"Microsoft has had two goals in the last 10 years. One was to copy the Mac, and the other was to copy Lotus' success in the spreadsheet – basically, the applications business. And over the course of the last 10 years, Microsoft accomplished both of those goals. And now they are completely lost. They were able to copy the Mac because the Mac was frozen in time. The Mac didn't change much for the last 10 years. It changed maybe 10 percent. It was a sitting duck. It's amazing that it took Microsoft 10 years to copy something that was a sitting duck."*

*Rolling Stone*, July 16, 1994.

*"Every once in a while a revolutionary product comes along that changes everything. It's very fortunate if you can work on just one of these in your career. Apple's been very fortunate in that it's introduced a few of these."*

*Msn.com*, Jan. 9, 2007.

*"[Design is] not just what it looks like and feels like. Design is how it works."*

*New York Times Magazine*, Nov. 30, 2003

*"The desktop computer industry is dead. Innovation has virtually ceased. Microsoft dominates with very little innovation. That's over. Apple lost. The desktop market has entered the dark ages, and it's going to be in the dark ages for the next 10 years, or certainly for the rest of this decade."*

Wired, Feb. 1996.

*"You've got to start with the customer experience and work back toward the technology – not the other way around."*

World Wide Developers Conference, May 1997

*"That's been one of my mantras – focus and simplicity. Simple can be harder than complex: you have to work hard to get your thinking clean to make it simple. But it's worth it in the end, because once you get there, you can move mountains."*

BusinessWeek, May 25, 1998.

*"We're always thinking about new markets we could enter, but it's only by saying no that you can concentrate on the things that are really important."*

BusinessWeek, Oct. 12 2004

*"You can't just ask customers what they want and then try to give that to them. By the time you get it built, they'll want something new."*

Inc. Magazine, April 1, 1989

# Bibliography

**Books about Apple**

The following references have relevance to Apple's historical facts.

[AME 15] AMES M., "Google begged Steve Jobs for permission to hire engineers for its new Paris office. Guess what happened next", available at: https://pando.com/2014/03/27/how-steve-jobs-forced-google-to-cancel-its-plan-to-open-a-paris-office/, July 2015.

[BEA 11] BEAHM G., *I, Steve: Steve Jobs in His Own Words*, B2 Books, Chicago, IL, 2011.

[BLU 12] BLUMENTHAL K., *Steve Jobs: the Man Who Thought Different*, Bloomsbury Publishing, London, 2012.

[COM 84] McCORMACK M.H., *What They Don't Teach You at Harvard Business School*, Collins, 1984.

[DOR 12] DORMEHL L., *The Apple Revolution: Steve Jobs, the Counterculture and How the Crazy Ones Took Over the World*, Virgin Books, Random House Group, 2012.

[EES 12] ESSANY M., *Steve Jobs: Ten Lessons in Leadership*, New Beginnings Press, Memphis, TN, 2012.

[ESL 13] ESSLINGER H., *Keep It Simple: the Early Design Years of Apple*, Arnoldsche Verlagsanstalt, 2013.

[GAL 09] GALLO C., *The Presentation Secrets of Steve Jobs: How to Be Insanely Great in Front of Any Audience*, McGraw-Hill, 2009.

[GAL 10] GALLO C., *The Innovation Secrets of Steve Jobs: Insanely Different Principles for Breakthrough Success*, McGraw-Hill, 2010.

[GAL 12] GALLO C., *The Apple Experience: Secrets of Building Insanely Great Customer Loyalty*, McGraw-Hill, New York, 2012.

[GAS 87] GASSEE J.L., *The Third Apple*, Harcourt Brace Jovanovitch, 1987.

[HER 04] HERTZFELD A., *Revolution in the Valley – How the Mac was Made*, OReilly, Sebastopol, CA, 2004.

[HUL 15] HULOT J.M., available at: https://en.wikipedia.org/wiki/Jean-Marie_Hullot, 2015.

[ISA 11] ISAACSON W., *Steve Jobs: The Exclusive Biography*, Simon & Shuster, 2011.

[ILI 15] ILIAN G., *Steve Jobs: 50 Life and Business Lessons from Steve Jobs*, Georgellian.com, 2015.

[JOH 15] JOHNSTON C., *Steve Jobs: 101 Greatest Business Lessons, Inspiration and Quotes From Steve Jobs*, Kindle Editions, 2015.

[KAH 13] KAHNEY L., *Jony Ive: the Genius Behind Apple's Greatest Products*, Penguin Group, New York, 2013.

[KAN 15] KANE Y.I., *Haunted Empire, Apple After Steve Jobs*, Harper Collins, New York, 2015.

[KAW 90] KAWASAKI G., *The Macintosh Way*, Harper Collins, 1990.

[LAS 12] LASHINSKY A., *Inside Apple – How America's Most Admired – and Secretive – Company Really Works*, Hachette Book Group. New York, 2012.

[LIN 04] LINZMAYER O.W., *Apple Confidential 2.0: The Definitive History of the World's Most Colorful Company: The Real Story of Apple Computer Inc.*, No Starch Press, San Francisco, CA, 2004.

[MEN 14] MENUES D., *Fearless Genius, the Digital Revolution in Silicon Valley*, Apple Store, 2014.

[PAT 15] PATERSON M., *Steve Jobs: 7 Top Life and Business Lessons of Steve Jobs for Unlimited Success*, Kindle Edition, 2015.

[SCH 15] SCHENDLER B., TETZELI R., *Becoming Steve Jobs: The evolution of a reckless upstart into a visionary leader*, Penguin Random House, New York, 2015.

[SEG 13] SEGALL K., *Insanely Simple: the Obsession That Drives Apples's Success*, Penguin Group, 2013.

[STA 04] STARKEY K., HATCHUEL A., TEMPEST S., "Rethinking the business school", *Journal of Management Studies*, vol. 41.8, pp. 1521–1531, 2004.

[TZU] TZU S., *The Art Of War*, available at: http://classics.mit.edu/Tzu/artwar.html.

[WOZ 06] WOZNIAK S., SMITH G., *I, WOZ: Computer Geek to Cult Icon – Getting to the Core of Apple's Inventor*, Headline Publishing Group, Hachette Livre, UK Ltd, London, 2006.

[ZUF 14] ZUFI J., ICONIC, *A Photographic Tribute to Apple Innovation*, 2nd Ed., http://iconicbook.com, 2014.

APPLE Inc. Wikipedia page provides ample historical information. Available at: https://en.wikipedia.org/wiki/Apple_Inc.

The Apple Distinguished Educators Programme is referenced at: https://www.apple.com/befr/education/apple-distinguished-educator/ [as of August 2015].

Ken Segall's Observatory: available at: kensegall.com/blog


## Complementary references

The following references have relevance either to the thinking behind Apple's historical facts, or to methods used in this book.

[ABE 78] ABERNATHY W., UTTERBACK J., "Patterns of industrial innovation", *Technology Review*, vol. 2, pp. 40–47, 1978.

[BBC 05] BBC News, *Our DNA hasn't changed, five questions to Steve Jobs*, available at http://archive.fortune.com/magazines/fortune/fortune_archive/2005/02/21/8251766/index.htm, 2005.

[COR 01] CORSI P., DULIEU M., *The Innovation Drive – The Marketing of Advanced Technologies*, Knowledge 2 Know-How, London, 2001.

[COR 06] CORSI P. *et al.* (eds), *Innovation Engineering: The Power of Intangible Networks*, ISTE, London, 2006.

[COR 08a] CORSI P., DULIEU M., *The Marketing of Technology Intensive Products and Services*, John Wiley & Sons, New York and ISTE, London, 2008.

[COR 08b] CORSI P., "Toward global assessment of innovative projects: the MagicEye method", *Journal of Futures Studies*, vol. 12, pp. 45–71, February 2008.

[COR 13] CORSI P., "A formal approach for designing creative futures based on C-K theory", *On the Horizon*, available at: http://www.emeraldinsight.com/oth.htm, vol. 21, no. 1, pp. 54–68, February 2013.

[COR 15] CORSI P., NEAU E., *Innovation Capability Maturity Model*, John Wiley & Sons, ISTE, London, and New York, June 2015.

[COR 15a] CORSI P., NEAU E., *Les dynamiques de l'innovation – modèles, méthodes et outils*, Hermes-Sciences, Lavoisier, Paris, 2011.

[COR 15b] CORSI P., "Forcing the design of fictional futures: from theory to cases implementation", *Journal of Futures Studies*, 2015 (publication pending).

[CRO 67] CROPLEY A.J., *Creativity*, Longman, London, 1967.

[CRO 05] CROPLEY A.J., "In praise of convergent thinking", *Creativity Research Journal*, vol. 18, pp. 391–404, 2005.

[CRO 15b] CROPLEY A.J., In praise of convergent thinking, University of Hamburg, 2015.

[DIA 05] DIAMOND J., *Collapse: How Societies Choose to Fail or Succeed*, Penguin Group, New York, 2005.

[DYM 95] DYMOND K.M., *A Guide to the CMM*, Process Inc., Annapolis, MD, 1995.

[FAB 15] FABIEN J., LE MASSON P., WEIL B., "Engage engineers as designers to generate new meanings in concept generation", *R&D Management Conference*, Pisa, Italy, June 2015.

[FRE 00] FREIBERGER P., *Fire in the Valley*, 2nd ed., McGraw-Hill Companies, 2000.

[GAY 15] GAY A., ANANDRAJ V. (eds), *Of Ordinary Men and Less Ordinary Leadership*, World Scientific, June 2015.

[GIG 10] GIGAND G., Se cultiver en complexité: la trialectique, un outil transdisciplinaire, Chronique Sociale, Lyon, France, 2010.

[GIG 15] GIGAND G., BRECHET J.P., *Le partiel, le partial, le parcellaire – L'intelligence trialectique de la complexité des phénomènes organisationnels*, Opéra, Editions Opéra, Nantes, France, 2015.

[HAT 03] HATCHUEL A., WEIL B., "A new approach of innovative design: an introduction to C-K design theory", *ICED 03*, Stockholm, The Design Society, 2003.

[HEI 30] HEISENBERG W., *Le manifeste de 1942*, Allia, Paris, 2003.

[HER 04] HERTZFELD A., *Revolution in the Valley: the Insanely Great Story of How the Mac was Made*, Sebastopol, CA: O'Reilly, 2004.

[HUL 13] HULLOT J.M., My iLife, available at https://www.youtube.com/watch?v=LLAWk-w0l-k&app=desktop, 2013. See also: https://fr.wikipedia.org/wiki/ Jean-Marie_Hullot.

[HUM 89] HUMPHREY W.S., *Managing the Software Process*, Addison-Wesley, Reading, MA, 1989.

[ILL 15] INSPIRING LIFE LESSONS, *Steve Jobs: 40 Leadership Life Lessons and Wisdom: an Inspiring Story Of Leadership*, Kindle Editions, 2015.

[KEN 13] KENNEDY D.S., *How to Succeed in Business by Breaking All the Rules*, BusinessNews Publishing, February 2013.

[KIM 05] KIM W.C., MAUBORGNE R., *Blue Ocean Strategy, How to Create Uncontested Market Space and Make the Competition Irrelevant*, Harvard Business School Press, 2005.

[MAR 15] MARION C., CHAUDRUC M.-C., "Leonardo Da Vinci and France", Château du Clos Lucé, Parc Léonardo da Vinci, 2015.

[MAS 06] MASSOTTE P., CORSI P., *La complexité dans les processus de management et de décision*, Hermes-Lavoisier, Paris, 2006.

[MAS 07] MASSOTTE P., CORSI P., *La gestion dynamique des risques économiques*, Hermes – Lavoisier, Paris, 2007.

[MAS 15a] MASSOTTE P., CORSI P., *Sustainability Calling – Underpinning Technologies*, ISTE, London and John Wiley & Sons, New York, September 2015.

[MAS 15b] MASSOTTE P., CORSI P., *Operationalizing Sustainability*, ISTE, London, and John Wiley & Sons, New York, September 2015.

[MOR 03] MORIN E., *Introduction à la pensée complexe*, le Seuil, Paris, 2003.

[MOR 04] MORIN E., *La Méthode*, 6 volumes: *La Nature de la nature, 1977; La Vie de la vie, 1980; La Connaissance de la connaissance, 1986; Les Idées, 1991; L'Humanité de l'humanité, 2001; L'Éthique complexe*, le Seuil, Paris, 2004.

[NAT 15] NATIONAL GEOGRAPHIC HISTORY, Leonardo Da Vinci – the scientific visionary, National Geographic, April–May 2013.

[PAS 65] PASCAL B., *Pensées*, Bordas, Paris, 1965.

[RIC 52] RICHTER I.A. (ed.), *Leonardo Da Vinci: Notebooks*, Oxford University Press, Oxford, 1952.

[RIC 08] RICHTER I.A. (ed.), *Leonardo Da Vinci: Notebooks*, Oxford University Press, Oxford, 2008.

[ROG 83] ROGERS E., *Diffusion of Innovations*, The Free Press, New York, 3rd ed., 1983.

[ROG 95] ROGERS E., *Diffusion of Innovations*, The Free Press, New York, 4th ed., 1995.

[SCH 52] SCHRÖDINGER E., Transformation and interpretation in quantum mechanics, Notes for the Dublin Seminar, 1952.

[SCR 15] SCRUM: Software management and control process, available at: https://www.scrum.org, 2015.

[TAN 92] TANAKE H., "Leonardo da Vinci, Architect of Chambord?", *Artibus et Historiae*, vol. 13, no. 25, pp. 85–102, 1992.

[TNT 99] T6996, TNT Originals Inc. Package Design, 1999. TNT Originals Inc. & Warner Bros Entertainment Inc., Warner Home Video Inc, warnervideo.com, Burbank, CA, 2005.

[TNT 99] FREIBERGER P., SWAINE M., Pirates of Silicon Valley – The True Story of How Bill Gates and Steve Jobs Changed the World, docudrama, warnervideo.com, tent.tv, T6996, TNT Originals Inc. Package Design, 1999.

[UTT 75] UTTERBACK J.L., ABERNATHY W.J., "A dynamic model of process and product, innovation, Omega", *The International Journal of Management Science*, vol. 3, no. 6, pp. 639–656, 1975.

[UTT 94] UTTERBACK J.M., *Mastering the Dynamics of Innovation*, Harvard Business School Press, Boston, MA, 1994, 1996.

The citations by John Lennon, an English musician, singer and songwriter (1940–1980) are intended for nonlinear thinking parallels with Steve Jobs.

## Sites of interest

http://fortune.com/2011/08/25/apples-core-who-does-what/
http://www.tuxboard.com/organigramme-de-google-facebook-microsoft-apple/

On Trialectics: http://www.complexitude.com/index.php?lang=en

## Further reading

[WIL 97] WILSON M., *The Difference Between God and Larry Elison (God Doesn't Think He's Larry Elison) – Inside Oracle Corporation*, Harper Business, 1997.

On C-K Theory. The effectiveness of using C-K design theory has been proven in many business and industrial contexts. For the readers interested in learning about it in an easy and highly illustrated way, the authors recommend the following eBooks series. More reading is included therein.

## References specific to Appendix 3

Citations are from Da Vinci unless referenced otherwise in the text.

[AGO 14] AGOGUE M., HOOGE S., ARNOUX F. *et al.*, *An Introduction to Innovative Design – Elements and Applications of C-K Theory*, Presses des Mines, Transvalor, Paris, 2014.

[ARA 98] ARASSE D., *Leonardo Da Vinci: The Rhythm of the World*, Konecky & Konecky, New York, 1998.

[BRA 91] BRAMLY S., *Leonardo: Discovering the Life of Leonardo Da Vinci*, Harper Collins, New York, 1991.

[CAP 07] CAPRA F., *The Science of Leonardo – Inside the Mind of the Great Genius of the Renaissance*, Doubleday, New York, 2007.

[COR 10] CORSI P., MATHIEU J.-P., RICHIR S., "Les codes méthodologiques de Léonard de Vinci – Impacts pour l'éducation et la recherche en réalitévirtuelle", *Revue Management et Sciences Sociales*, MSS, vol. 5, no. 8, pp. 9–26, January–June, 2010.

[GAL 98a] GALLUZZI P. (ed.), *La mente di Leonardo –Nel laboratorio del genio universal*, Giunti, Firenze, 1998.

[GAL 98b] GELB M., *How to Think like Leonardo Da Vinci, Seven Steps to Genius Everyday*, Delacorte Press, New York, 1998.

[HAT 04] HATCHUEL A., LE MASSON P., WEIL B., "C-K theory in practice: lessons from industrial applications", *International Design Conference – DESIGN 2004*, Dubrovnik: FMENA University of Zagreb/The Design Society, May 18-21, 2004.

[HAT 09] HATCHUEL A., WEIL B., "C-K design theory: an advanced formulation", *Research in Engineering Design*, vol. 19, pp. 181–192, 2009.

[HOP 01] HOPE C., *The Last 'Last Supper'*, New York Review of Books, August 9, 2001.

[KEM 81] KEMP M., *Leonardo Da Vinci: The Marvelous Works of Nature and Man*, Harvard University Press, Cambridge, Mass, 1981.

[KOK 13] KOKSHAGINA O., LE MASSON P., WEIL B. *et al.*, "How design theories enable the design of generic technologies: notion of generic concept and genericity improvement", *ICED 2013*, August 19–22, Seoul, Korea, 2013.

[KOK 14] KOKSHAGINA O., Risk management in double unknown: theory, model and organization for the design of generic technologies, Ecole Nationale Supérieure des Mines de Paris, 2014.

[LEM 10] LE MASSON P., HATCHUEL A., WEIL B., *Strategic Management of Innovation and Design*, Cambridge University Press, Cambridge, 2010.

[LEM 12] LE MASSON P., WEIL B., "Design theories as languages of the unknown: insights from the German roots of systematic design (1840–1960)", *Research in Engineering Design*, 2012.

[PED 07] PEDRETTI C., Personal communications from ex-Armand Hammer Chair Professor of Leonardo Studies Emeritus at UCLA, Los Angeles, available at: http://www.librarything.fr/author/pedretticarlo, 2007–2010.

[RIC 98] RICHTER I.A. (ed.), *The Notebooks of Leonardo Da Vinci*, Oxford University Press, Oxford, 1998.

[ROS 02] ROSS S., *Leonardo Da Vinci, Scientists Who Made History Series*, Raintree Steck-Vaughn Austin, TX., 2002.

[SCH 15] SCHLENDER B., TETZELL R., "Becoming Steve Jobs – How a reckless upstart became a visionaly leader", Sceptre, Hodder & Stoughton, Hachette, UK, 2015.

[SIM 89] SIMON H.A., KULKARNI D., *The Process of Scientific Discovery: The Strategy of Experimentation*, Yale University Press, 1989.

[VEZ 06] VEZZOZI A., SABATO A., Leonardo mito e verità. Riscoperte, attualitàe nodi della conoscenza. Museo Ideale Leonardo Da Vinci, Vinci (Firenze), available at: www.museoLeonardo.it, 2006.

[ZÖL 03] ZÖLLNER F., *Leonardo da Vinvi*, Taschen GmbH, Cologne, 2003.

## Other references

[TOU 12] Touchpress Limited, *Anatomy,* available at: https://appsto.re/fr/g1YbF.i, 2012-2015. Stunning app that visualizes a Leonardo da Vinci's drawings Apple Store, collection from the Royal Collection of Her Majesty Queen Elizabeth II at Windsor Castle. Even amazing to see the natively genuine design fit between an iPad and the drawings.

www.universalleonardo.org

legacy.mos.org/Leonardo/

# Index

## A, B, C

acquisition, 28, 42, 43, 46, 51–53, 100, 107

activities, 52, 57

analogy, 107

antagonism, 4, 71, 94

anticipation, 114, 117, 123

Apple university, 118, 119

Apple's failures, 10

artifacts, 95, 120

assets, 51, 53, 104

attractor, 113, 114

bill gates, 12, 27

biodesign, 87

brainstorming, 92

branding, 79

breaking axis, 4

business
    domains
    school, 4, 34, 40, 63, 71–79, 85, 90
    process reengineering, 120

C-K
    diagram, 105, 109, 110, 115
    theory, 10, 11, 103, 105, 107, 113, 120, 125

cannibalization, 8

capability maturity model (CMM), 11, 124

categories (products), 30

Chutzpah, 11–13, 99

CMM model, 11, 124

code, 57–59, 118

coding, 58

coherency, 18, 117, 119, 125

comfort zone, 74

commercial policy, 71

communication, 74

competencies, 104, 105, 117

competitiveness, 102, 103, 105, 107, 110, 120, 125

complexity, 4, 19, 40, 81, 119

concept
    generation, 92

connecting (the) dots, 19

consciousness, 63, 90, 91, 94, 95, 121

content, 8, 85

crazy concept, 91, 95, 105

creativity, 28, 64, 79, 81, 84, 89, 90, 92, 109

cultural bias, 3, 4

culture, 4, 34, 35, 117, 119, 124, 125

customer experience, 17, 40, 71, 72

## D, E, F

degree, 56, 113, 118
developers, 15, 85
differentiation, 75, 110
digital corp., 34
discipline, 56, 79
disruptive mentality, 127
dominant designs, 92, 103–105
dominant thinking, 94
dots, 19, 87, 93
double helix, 84
dualistic views, 93
Eastern vs Western culture, 126
Ecole Normale Supérieure (ENS), 57
ecosystem, 32, 46, 52, 87, 93, 94, 114,
    117, 119
engineering, 56, 81, 86, 94, 126
entanglement, 93
erasmus, 93
escher, 87
eureka moments, 10
experimentation, 96
failure, 63
fear quotient, 10
fiascos, 64
fights, 28
firm, 4, 5, 40, 41, 81, 85, 86, 91, 104,
    105, 118–120, 123–125
fixations, 4
focus group(s), 92, 120
fonts, 19
foresight, 119
form factor, 17, 67, 69

## G, H, I

G4 Cube, 67, 69
genes, 3, 4, 10, 13, 25, 34, 70, 74, 99,
    123-126
genetic engineering, 27
gradient, 114, 115, 123

growing returns, 116
guy kawasaki, 11, 126
hardware, 55, 102
hemispheric balance, 86
holistic, 93, 94
hologram, 93
HTC, 18
humanities, 126
IBM, 12, 13, 27, 39, 65, 85
iBooks Author, 93
iCloud, 48, 49, 51
impact, 41, 43, 113, 114, 118, 119
incompleteness, 95, 114
indeterminacy, 96, 113
innovation
    capability maturity model, 11, 124
    fields, 125
    molecule, 123–125
innovativeness, 103, 104, 113
intuition, 23, 93, 126
iPad, 8, 19, 24, 35, 82, 91
iPhone, 3, 8, 17, 24, 30, 82, 88, 96
iTunes, 9, 24, 26, 66, 87, 88, 91
iWorks, 26

## J, K, L

Jean-Marie Hullot, 57, 58
John Lennon, 3
Jony Ive, 16, 17, 88
Ken Segall, 19
Keynotes, 77
Knowledge bandwidth, 95
Kodak, 68
leader, 11, 36, 37, 79, 80, 88
leadership, 102
learning, 4, 33, 94, 95
legacy, 25, 109, 118
Leonardo Da Vinci, 10, 31, 84, 86, 88,
    90, 91, 93, 94, 125
lever, 118

liberal arts, 126
lineage, 127
linear
   structure, 3
   thinking, 89, 119
Lisa, 35, 64, 65

## M, N, O

Mac Pro, 36
Macintosh, 11, 35, 65–67, 69, 70, 86
Macintosh TV, 35, 66, 69
MagicEye diagram, 117, 119
make or buy strategy, 41
mantra inside, 74
maps, 52
marker event, 92
market share, 16, 24, 26, 30, 35, 46, 71,
   80, 104
market studies, 22, 23, 126
marketing, 9, 11, 23, 35, 40, 67, 76, 79
MBA, 8, 28, 56
me-too supplier, 100
Meg Whitman, 16
mental constructs, 4
metaphors, 4, 19, 64
methodology/methodologies, 81, 95, 103,
   104
Michelangelo, 59
microsoft, 26–28, 31, 34, 35, 43, 68, 73
mines paristech, 10
minimalist, 17
mistakes, 34
mobile, 24, 27, 30, 35, 57, 73
models, 68, 87, 119
montaigne, 93
multidimensional, 95, 101, 117, 120
nature, 18, 52, 56, 57, 63, 93
netscape, 31
Newton, 26, 35, 65, 66, 68
NeXT, 19, 52, 57, 59
Nikola Tesla, 3

Nokia Communicator, 18
objectives, 29, 31, 118
object identity, 57, 73
office, 24, 26–28, 30, 34, 35, 58
opportunity, 10, 26, 29
oracle, 26
outside the box, 4
outsource, 41

## P, Q, R, S

pages, 93
perseverance, 36
pippin, 35, 68, 69
product design, 15
programmers, 57–59
project management, 31
purpose, 30, 31, 51, 80, 95, 105, 114
quantum, 86, 87, 93, 120, 126
   physics, 86
   property, 87
QuickTake 100 camera, 67, 68
Raymond Loewy, 16
RDF, 89, 90
reality, 4, 7, 73, 89
   distortion field (RDF), 89
renaissance, 120
research and development, 39
resilience, 31
risk-taking, 125–127
risks, 8, 30, 35, 125
rules, 4, 75, 92, 123
scheduling, 96
Sfumato, 90
skills, 4, 104, 105
spec. sheet, 17
stakeholders, 118
start-up, 34, 42, 46
Stephen Covey, 126
structure, 3, 42, 75, 76, 85
sustainability, 4, 31, 119
systemic thinking, 87

## T, U, V, W, Z

talents, 105
thinking way, 86, 120
thought engineering, 81
transdisciplinarity, 81, 87

trialectics, 81, 96, 107–109, 111. 113, 114, 120
undecidable, 105, 114
user experience, 17, 110
variety, 23, 28
whole brand, 125
Zen-spirit, 17

Other titles from

in

Innovation, Entrepreneurship and Management

## 2015

CASADELLA Vanessa, LIU Zeting, DIMITRI Uzunidis
*Innovation Capabilities and Economic Development in Open Economies*

CORSI Patrick, NEAU Erwan
*Innovation Capability Maturity Model*

MAILLARD Pierre
*Competitive Quality and Innovation*

MASSOTTE Pierre, CORSI Patrick
*Sustainability Calling*

MASSOTTE Pierre, CORSI Patrick
*Operationalizing Sustainability*

## 2014

DUBÉ Jean, LEGROS Diègo
*Spatial Econometrics Using Microdata*

LESCA Humbert, LESCA Nicolas
*Strategic Decisions and Weak Signals*

## 2013

HABART-CORLOSQUET Marine, JANSSEN Jacques, MANCA Raimondo
*VaR Methodology for Non-Gaussian Finance*

## 2012

DAL PONT Jean-Pierre
*Process Engineering and Industrial Management*

MAILLARD Pierre
*Competitive Quality Strategies*

POMEROL Jean-Charles
*Decision-Making and Action*

SZYLAR Christian
*UCITS Handbook*

## 2011

LESCA Nicolas
*Environmental Scanning and Sustainable Development*

LESCA Nicolas, LESCA Humbert
*Weak Signals for Strategic Intelligence: Anticipation Tool for Managers*

MERCIER-LAURENT Eunika
*Innovation Ecosystems*

## 2010

SZYLAR Christian
*Risk Management under UCITS III/IV*

## 2009

COHEN Corine
*Business Intelligence*

ZANINETTI Jean-Marc
*Sustainable Development in the USA*

## 2008

CORSI Patrick, DULIEU Mike
*The Marketing of Technology Intensive Products and Services*

DZEVER Sam, JAUSSAUD Jacques, ANDREOSSO Bernadette
*Evolving Corporate Structures and Cultures in Asia / Impact of Globalization*

## 2007

AMMI Chantal
*Global Consumer Behavior*

## 2006

BOUGHZALA Imed, ERMINE Jean-Louis
*Trends in Enterprise Knowledge Management*

CORSI Patrick *et al.*
*Innovation Engineering: the Power of Intangible Networks*

CPSIA information can be obtained at www.ICGtesting.com
Printed in the USA
BVOW06*2300020216

435243BV00008B/14/P